NEW
GLASS
NOW

40th-Anniversary Issue of
NEW GLASS REVIEW

THE CORNING MUSEUM OF GLASS

Corning, New York
2019

New Glass Now celebrates 40 years of *New Glass Review*, an annual exhibition-in-print featuring 100 of the most timely, innovative projects in glass. It is curated from an open call for submissions by the curator of modern and contemporary glass at The Corning Museum of Glass and a changing panel of guest curators.

This publication is accompanied by the exhibitions "New Glass Now" and "New Glass Now: Context," held at The Corning Museum of Glass from May 12, 2019, to January 5, 2020.

THIS YEAR'S CURATORS WERE:

ARIC CHEN (AC)
Curator-at-Large
M+ (museum for visual culture)
Hong Kong SAR, China

SUSANNE JØKER JOHNSEN (SJJ)
Head of Exhibitions
The Royal Danish Academy of Fine Arts
Schools of Architecture, Design,
  and Conservation
Copenhagen, Denmark

BETH LIPMAN (BL)
Artist
Sheboygan Falls, Wisconsin

SUSIE J. SILBERT (SJS)
Curator of Modern and Contemporary Glass
The Corning Museum of Glass

In 2018, a total of 1,433 individuals and companies from 53 countries submitted 3,754 digital images. All entries, including those that were not selected for publication, are archived in the Museum's Rakow Research Library.

The entry form is available at
www.cmog.org/newglassreview.

All objects reproduced in this *Review* were chosen with the understanding that they were designed and made between 2015 and 2018.

Unless otherwise noted, all photographs in the "New Glass Now" section are courtesy of the artists.

All dimensions are height x width x depth.

Additional copies are available at shops.cmog.org.

HEAD OF PUBLICATIONS
Richard W. Price

EDITOR
Susie J. Silbert

DESIGN AND PRODUCTION
Jacolyn Saunders

CONTRIBUTING EDITORS
Whitney Birkett
Violet Wilson

DIGITAL SUBMISSIONS
Brian Hewitt
Mandy Kritzeck
Ryan Langille
Michelle Padilla

MARKETING AND COMMUNICATIONS
Ann Campbell
Theresa Cornelissen
Amanda Sterling
Kimberly Thompson

MUSEUM PHOTOGRAPHERS
Bryan H. Buchanan
Andrew Fortune
Allison Lavine
Marty Pierce

AUDIOVISUAL
Scott Ignaszewski
Jason Thayer
Matt Wilbur

RIGHTS AND REPRODUCTIONS
Lori Fuller
Suzanne Abrams Rebillard

Additional thanks to:
Mary Chervenak, Emily Davis, Alexandra Ruggiero, Linnea Seidling, James Truxon, and all of the artists, designers, collectors, and institutions that submitted images to be considered for *New Glass Review*.

Standard Book Number: 978-0-87290-218-3

ISSN: 0275:469X

Library of Congress Control Number: 81-641214

New Glass Review is printed by AGS Custom Graphics in Macedonia, Ohio, and distributed with *GLASS: The UrbanGlass Art Quarterly* magazine, published by UrbanGlass, New York, New York. It is also available as a separate volume.

NEW GLASS is not NEW

As a concept and an initiative, "New Glass" has existed for 60 years.

The brainchild of Thomas S. Buechner, founding director of The Corning Museum of Glass, New Glass originated in the mid-1950s, just a few years after the Museum was chartered. It first appeared in "Glass 1959," the first major museum exhibition of international contemporary glass in the world. Twenty years later, the exhibition "New Glass: A Worldwide Survey" reignited the initiative, followed directly by the inauguration of *New Glass Review*, an annual exhibition-in-print whose 40th-anniversary issue you hold in your hand. Each of these projects, and the free exchange of information they enabled, contributed to the growth of contemporary glass, helping it to become the dynamic, innovative, global field it is today. It is our hope that this most recent iteration of New Glass—the exhibition and exhibition-in-print "New Glass Now"—will contribute in a similar way, providing a framework, a bridge to the future of the field.

At its core, New Glass is founded on the belief that contemporary glass is an evolving organism, one that needs to be seen in order to grow. To that end, New Glass has employed a remarkably democratic selection process that over the last 60 years has coalesced into what can be termed "The New Glass Model." This model consists of an international open call for submissions, the responses of self-nominating artists, and a panel of diverse thought leaders in art, craft, and design who review and select from them. Uniquely, the panel does not make its selections through full consensus. Instead, the two-day, four-round process encourages each panelist to develop and deploy his or her own criteria, in conversation with fellow panelists. During the first three rounds, the group winnows the selections together. In the final round, each panelist individually selects 25 pieces from the remaining pool, until 100 have been identified. Once the final 100 have been picked, other panelists can add their names to the works, so that individual voices are layered atop one another in many but not all cases.

Since the inception of New Glass, the Museum has made these individual selections transparent to the public, typically by publishing the selector's (or selectors') initials alongside the printed images in the catalog or *Review*. This transparency is central to the New Glass method and, combined with the method's heterogeneous decision making, means that each New Glass project is necessarily diverse in viewpoint and transparent in a way that few curatorial projects are. To continue and extend this legacy, in *New Glass Review 39*, I added bylined statements from the panelists to all of the pieces in the publication. We have opted to include these statements, as well as the initials of each selector, to the gallery labels in "New Glass Now" to emphasize the layered perspectives that shaped the exhibition.

NEW GLASS: CONTEXT

The story of New Glass begins with "Glass 1959." The 1950s were a design-focused time, and the exhibition reflected this—from the

The "Glass 1959" jurors reviewing object submissions. *Left to right*: Axel von Saldern, George Nakashima, Leslie Cheek, Russell Lynes, and Edgar Kaufmann Jr. (Gio Ponti is not pictured), 1959.

"Glass 1959" installation with visitors at The Corning Museum of Glass, 1959.

Head I by Stanislav Libenský and Jaroslava Brychtová (62.3.132). Featured in "Glass 1959."

"New Glass: A Worldwide Survey" installation at The Corning Museum of Glass, 1979.

panelists to the works they selected. A few of the selections, however, were significant sculptural works by individual designer-craftsmen and -women. Notably, "Glass 1959" marked the first American display of work by the pioneering Czech artists Jaroslava Brychtová and Stanislav Libenský. The show was a breakthrough for the field, allowing artists, designers, enthusiasts, and the general public alike to see global glass production en masse for the first time. Seeing so much work in one place demonstrated the possibilities of the material to an audience with a growing hunger to adapt glass in service of individual expression. It is no wonder that the Studio Glass movement emerged just a few years later.

Twenty years on, again under the direction of Thomas S. Buechner, the Museum renewed the New Glass initiative with another international exhibition of contemporary glass. By this time, the Studio Glass movement was in full swing and the glass world had changed immeasurably. "New Glass: A Worldwide Survey" was based on the same model as "Glass 1959," but it took place in a profoundly new context, one that embraced art and lauded the individual. Whereas the vast majority of objects in the 1959 show were produced by firms, by 1979 only a few were. Instead, nearly all of the entries came from artists working directly with the material.

Ever ambitious in scope, "New Glass: A Worldwide Survey" traveled across the United States and to three international venues. As a result of this travel, the widespread distribution of its catalog, and significant press coverage (including a feature story in *Life* magazine), more people saw—and became involved in—contemporary glass than ever before. Cultural heritage institutions and private individuals started collecting glass, new artists began working in glass (including Kirstie Rea, featured on pages 40–41), and more publications devoted space to articles on the material and its makers.

Individually, both "Glass 1959" and "New Glass: A Worldwide Survey" catalyzed incredible changes in the field and conveyed prestige on new generations of artists and designers. Recognizing the power of these exhibitions to accelerate the growth of the field, the Museum launched New Glass Review, the third and longest-lived expression of the New Glass concept. The idea for the Review originated in a 1975 meeting, organized by Buechner, which brought together leading voices of studio glass, the influential director and craft thinker Paul

Smith, and designers from Steuben Glass to discuss the Museum's role in furthering the Studio Glass movement.[1]

Of the many initiatives discussed at the meeting, the desire for a "slide archive with regular distribution or set sale arrangement" was the first to be put in place.[2] For three years, beginning in 1976, the museum published *Contemporary Art Glass*, a survey of contemporary glass released on microfiche only. *Contemporary Art Glass* beta-tested the concept of New Glass as an exhibition-in-print, and in 1980, following its success and that of "New Glass: A Worldwide Survey" and its catalog (both initiatives of the 1975 meeting), *New Glass Review* was born.

Since then, *New Glass Review* has featured 100 works by artists, designers, and craftspeople around the globe on an annual basis. Designed to give readers an insight into the ever-shifting landscape of contemporary glass, each issue of *New Glass Review* is made using the same democratic processes as the earlier exhibitions, with one notable exception: each year, the Museum's sitting curator of modern and contemporary glass chairs the panel, selects fellow panelists, and edits the publication. From 1980 to 1985, William Warmus oversaw *New Glass Review*, followed by Susanne Frantz (1987–1999) and Tina Oldknow (2000–2015). Since 2016, I have directed this effort. Each curator brought his or her own concerns to the publication, shaping it in an individual image while remaining true

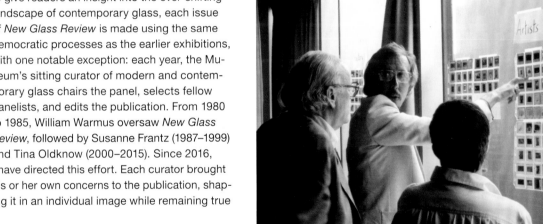

1. "The Corning Museum of Glass Contemporary Glass Artists Conference," *Glass Art Magazine*, v. 3, no. 2, April 1975, pp. 8–9. Among those in attendance were leaders of the Studio Glass movement, including Andre Billeci, James Carpenter, Dale Chihuly, Fritz Dreisbach, Henry Halem, Tom Kekic, Dominick Labino, Albert Lewis, Marvin Lipofsky, Harvey Littleton, Tom McGlauchlin, and Joel Philip Myers; Paul Smith, then director of the Museum of Contemporary Craft in New York City; and designers from Steuben Glass, including Eric Hilton and Paul Schulze.

2. Henry Halem, an attendee at the meeting, captured the initialed list of initiatives discussed in a photograph that he shared with the author on December 21, 2018.

Participants in the 1975 Studio Glass movement meeting in Corning. (Photo: Henry Halem)

"New Glass: A Worldwide Survey" jurors Werner Schmalenbach, Paul Smith, and Franca Santi Gualteri reviewing slide submissions.

Crystal Glass Sculpture by Pavel Hlava (78.3.50). Featured in "New Glass: A Worldwide Survey" (1979), selected by all jurors: Franca Santi Gualteri, Russell Lynes, Werner Schmalenbach, and Paul Smith.

The 100 works that make up "New Glass Now" are a sampling of the diverse visions and intersectional interests of a new generation of glassmakers and -workers who have forged their material exploration in a time of diverse inputs and possibilities. There are works in this exhibition that one could imagine, with little alteration, being included in "Glass 1959" or "New Glass: A Worldwide Survey," and others that could have been dreamed of only today. But whatever their reference—in material, technique, or concept— the works included in the following pages represent the breadth of contemporary glass.

To build a framework for this new material and to make sense of this abundant diversity, I have organized the work into six thematic areas—: in situ, : (infra)structures, : body politic, : embodied knowledge, : 01100111 01101100 01110011, and : phenomena. These are only ideas. They should be viewed as beginnings, frames, conversation starters. New Glass has always been about starting conversations and enabling a diverse panel and a diverse audience to have an opinion. Now it is your turn. Help us build the future of glass.

New Glass Now.

to the format and method. Thomas S. Buechner also remained an important influencer of the New Glass process he had initiated, sitting on every selection panel from 1980 through 2001.

NEW GLASS NOW

Each iteration of the New Glass concept has fundamentally altered the way glass was made, thought about, and understood. Reflecting the topical concerns of the era in which they were cast, and spurring growth in the discourse that followed, "Glass 1959," "New Glass: A Worldwide Survey," and *New Glass Review* built the contemporary glass world we see today. Now, we stand on the threshold of another change, one that pays homage to the past but builds in a new direction.

ACKNOWLEDGMENTS

This volume is dedicated to:

All who think and work in glass,
you are why we do this.

Dorothy Saxe, who has inspired so many,
and whose own story of New Glass 1979
gave shape to this catalog.

And Thomas S. Buechner, who showed
us the way.

The exhibition "New Glass Now," as well as its companion exhibit "New Glass Now: Context" on view in the Rakow Research Library, would have remained a kernel of an idea if not for the support of so many in the glass community. Without the enthusiastic submissions—past and present—of artists and designers around the globe, there would be no New Glass. Thank you for putting yourself and your work out there. I am grateful to Dorothy Saxe, Daniel P. and Welmoet B. van Kammen (in memory of Marleen van Kammen), Barbara and Dennis DuBois, and Kendra and Tom Kasten for their financial and intellectual support. I am honored to work in a field with so many truly visionary supporters.

Inside the Museum, Dr. Karol B. Wight, president and executive director, provided the leadership and advocacy to make this project grow. Carole Ann Fabian, director of collections, joined the Museum at a critical time in the project's development; it is stronger for her guidance. The exhibitions' core team consisted of Warren Bunn, collections and exhibitions manager; Kris Wetterlund, director of education and interpretation; Colleen McFarland Rademaker, associate librarian, special collections, and co-curator of "New Glass Now: Context"; and Troy Smythe, education and interpretation supervisor. Linnea Seidling, curatorial assistant, was essential to this project.

A number of curatorial interns helped to realize "New Glass Now: Context." I am deeply grateful for the work of Patricia Gomes over two summers (one generously funded by a Windgate Internship from The Center for Craft in Asheville, North Carolina), of Anna Millers, and of the inimitable Sarah Darro. Each is a gifted scholar who made significant contributions to the show.

Much of the success of "New Glass Now" and "New Glass Now: Context" rests with our incredible Collections Department. Our preparators, led by Robin Adornato, are conscientious, interested, and exceptionally skilled. Robin, Stephen Hazlett, David Kuentz, Lindsay Milano, and Thomas Oberg, thank you. Our registrars, led by Brandy Harold, brought a mind-boggling level of logistical creativity to this complex project. Special thanks to Emily Smith, assistant registrar, loans, for the feat of coordinating

agreements with more than 100 private lenders. Lianne Uesato, assistant conservator, is an important thought partner willing to embrace the challenges posed by experimental objects.

Major exhibitions always draw on the expertise of departments across the Museum's campus, and this was especially true for "New Glass Now." Among the many people who contributed to this project, Ann Campbell from Marketing and Communications, Lindsay Hahnes from Advancement, and Scott Ignaszewski from Programs and Events brought unparalleled drive and vision to planning the opening-weekend events. Courtney DeRusha and Rob Cassetti were instrumental in envisioning and implementing in-Museum graphics. The cross-departmental interpretive and logistics teams—cornerstones of the Museum's approach to exhibitions—provided critical input and were essential in threading the exhibitions' themes throughout the Museum campus. In addition to those already mentioned above or named on the title verso, these teams included Meghan Bunnell, Eric Goldschmidt, Evan Hill, Joeliene Magoto, and Kalli Snodgrass.

Additional funding for the exhibition came from the New York State Council on the Arts, the G & H Snyder Memorial Trust, and VISA Inc.

Full acknowledgments for the publication New Glass Now/New Glass Review 40 are on the title verso. However, additional thanks must go to our exceptionally gifted editor, Richard W. Price, head of publications; to Jacolyn Saunders, publications designer; and to Violet Wilson, senior administrative assistant. New Glass Review would not be the same without you.

Finally, special thanks to Dick Moiel and Kathy Poeppel, Mark Peiser, Cindi Strauss, Anna Walker, and Jeff Toohig. I wouldn't be here without you.

SUSIE J. SILBERT
Curator of Modern and Contemporary Glass
The Corning Museum of Glass

Geographic Distribution

:in situ

made
from place
reflecting
place making
place

MIYA ANDO

ATELIER NL
Lonny van Ryswyck
Nadine Sterk

ANS BAKKER

SARAH BRILAND

NACHO CARBONELL

ANDREA DA PONTE

SACHI FUJIKAKE

JEFF GOODMAN
and Jeff Goodman Studio

HANNA HANSDOTTER
for Kosta Boda

DAFNA KAFFEMAN

CAROLINE LANDAU

JAMES MAGAGULA
and Ngwenya Glass

KIRSTIE REA

CHIEMI WATANABE

IDA WIETH

TOOTS ZYNSKY

MIYA ANDO

United States (b. 1978)

Kumo (Cloud) for Glass House (Shizen), Nature Series

Etched glass

10.2 x 10.2 x 10.2 cm

AC, SJJ, SJS

Ando's ethereal, laser-etched paperweight was designed as a high-end souvenir of Philip Johnson's Glass House. Airy, reflective, and small enough to hold in your hands, *Kumo* is a tangible representation of the way it feels to be in the presence of Johnson's all-glass masterpiece. As such, it is a subtle and profound play on the souvenir as a reminder of a particular place, experience, and time.   *— SJS*

ATELIER NL

LONNY VAN RYSWYCK

The Netherlands (b. 1978)

and NADINE STERK

The Netherlands (b. 1977)

"ZandGlas – Savelsbos"
Cups, Decanter, and Test Crucibles

Blown glass and melted glass made from
sand collected from Savelsbos, Maastricht,
the Netherlands

Decanter: 23 x 10 cm
Crucibles: 4 x 6.5 x 6.5 cm

Photo: Blickfänger

AC, SJJ, BL, SJS

The design duo Atelier NL make glassware
that embodies the essence of place. They
start with the raw material, making their own
glass from sand harvested from a single
location. The final products are colored only
by the specific elements in that sand, so that
each series—each different glass formulated—
captures and makes visible the specific qualities
of its origin. — *SJS*

ANS BAKKER

The Netherlands (b. 1963)

Zeeuws Licht no. 1/The Light from Zeeland

Glass blown in sand molds

26 x 27 x 27 cm

Photo: Johan Kole

AC, SJJ, SJS

Bakker made *The Light from Zeeland* with the immediacy of a high tide rolling into the shore. To create the mottled surface of this piece, she made a blow mold out of wet sand impressed with rocks, seaweed, and oyster shells. These elements give her work an intuitive, almost naive appearance, but they also serve as a metacommentary on the formula of soda-lime glass, in which the sand stands in for silica, the oyster shells for lime, the seaweed for flux, and the rocks for color. — *SJS*

SARAH BRILAND

United States (b. 1980)

Problematica (Foam Rock)

Foam, Aqua Resin, glass microspheres,
steel, concrete stand

30.5 x 53 x 35 cm

Photo: Terry Brown

AC, BL, SJS

Touching on how plastics and other outputs
of human activity have irrevocably altered the
planet, Sarah Briland casts foam and other
synthetic materials in glass, imagining
them as future fossils in the epoch of the
Anthropocene.   *— AC*

NACHO CARBONELL

Spain (b. 1980)

El Patio

Fused and slumped glass; steel, barley paste, hardener

300 x 200 x 100 cm

AC, SJS

Nacho Carbonell's work often takes on an element of fantasy, as if his furniture designs were living organisms inhabiting a pixie dust–covered forest. Commissioned by a beer company in Granada, Spain, his *El Patio* installation joins two people beneath a stained glass canopy, casting light in recycled beer-bottle green. — AC

ANDREA DA PONTE

Argentina (b. 1967)

Globalized

Blown glass; transferred image

30 x 30 x 30 cm

Photo: Rosana Silvera

AC, SJS

Through her use of image transfer—specifically, using historical maps—on blown glass, Da Ponte creates a new cartographic projection, one that reminds us of how our expansionist relationship with geography and the planet often strains a more finite reality.   — AC

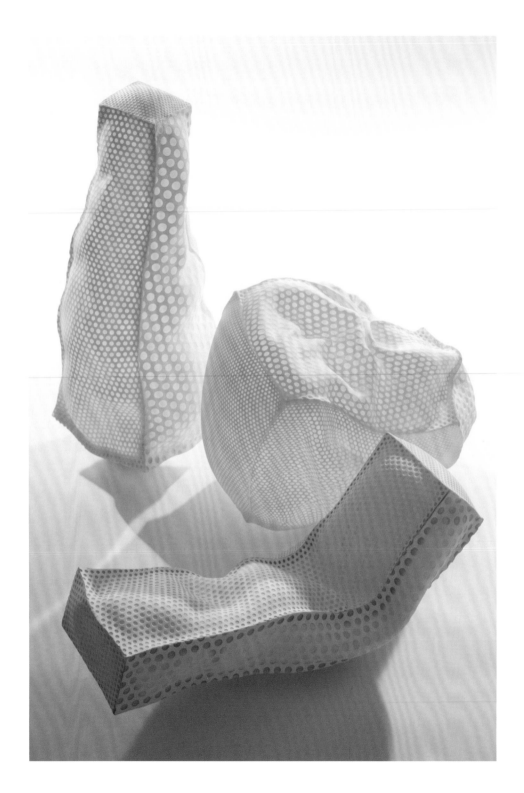

SACHI FUJIKAKE

Japan (b. 1985)

Vestige

Blown glass, sandblasted, cold-worked

Largest: 39 × 39 × 33 cm

AC, SJS

Fujikake's sculptures defy all material expec-
tations. They appear soft, featherweight, and
effortless, belying entirely the heat of their
construction and the incredible craftsmanship
used in their manufacture.   *—SJS*

JEFF GOODMAN
Canada (1961–2012)
and JEFF GOODMAN STUDIO

The Bahá'í Temple of South America

Hariri Pontarini Architects

Exterior tiles: kiln-cast borosilicate glass

Photo: Sebastian Wilson

AC, SJJ, BL, SJS

At first glance, one could think that this is a one-of-a-kind craft object, skillfully made with attention to detail, materiality, and form. Instead, it is a full-scale building and the result of a collaboration between architects and crafts-men. Goodman and the design team at his studio (following his death) have added their craftsmanship and soft sense of materiality, proportion, and object character to designing and fabricating the exterior panels of this architectural project.   *— SJJ*

HANNA HANSDOTTER

Sweden (b. 1984)

for KOSTA BODA Sweden

"Nightfall" Dome and Tower

Blown glass

Left: 27 x 25 x 25 cm
Right: 35.5 x 12.5 x 12.5 cm

SJJ, BL, SJS

In these lidded jars, one Swedish designer pays homage to another. Hansdotter was looking to Monica Backström and *Space*, her series of mirrored objects from the 1980s. Both were produced on assignment from Kosta Boda.   *– SJJ*

אם צמח מולדת אתה ורצונך

לחסות בחיקה, –אהב   אותה

וחיה אותה- בהר ובגיא, בצמח ובחי.

DAFNA KAFFEMAN

Israel (b. 1972)

If You Thirst for a Homeland and Seek Shelter in Its Bosom, Love It and Live in Its Mountains and Valleys, Its Flora and Fauna

Flameworked glass plants; black letter set, white felt

67 x 60 x 19 cm

Photo: Eric Tschernow, courtesy of lorch + seidel contemporary, and AIDA−Association of Israel's Decorative Arts

AC, SJJ, BL, SJS

In this herbarium assemblage, based on a 1965 field guide to Israeli plants, Kaffeman gives us a poetic introduction to the flora, geography, and history of Israel. The choice of plants and twigs, replicated in glass and placed on a soft felt background alongside quotes from the field guide, reaches into her motherland's cultural practice of commemoration, sacrifice, and mourning.

Kaffeman has occasionally shown these delicate objects with works that reproduce the horrific confession of an Israeli teenager involved in the retaliatory murder of a Palestinian one. Paired in that way, the fragility of the glass botanicals emphasizes the fragility of all life and the complexity of contemporary Israel.   — *SJJ*

CAROLINE LANDAU

United States (b. 1991)

Archiving Ice

Mold-blown glass; glacier water

7.6 x 19.7 x 14 cm

Project assistant: Maria Enomoto

Photo: Jennifer Hagan

AC

During an artist residency on the Svalbard archipelago, near the Arctic Circle, Caroline Landau used wax to cover chunks of ice that had washed ashore. The wax was later turned into molds for these blown glass vessels, which now serve as relics of the rapidly melting Arctic. — *AC*

JAMES MAGAGULA (b. 1964)
and NGWENYA GLASS
Kingdom of eSwatini (formerly Swaziland)

The Chief Herdsman and His Cattle

Hot-sculpted glass

30 x 60 x 70 cm

Photo: Ben Taylor

AC, SJJ, BL, SJS

Magagula, one of the head glassblowers at
Ngwenya Glass in eSwatini (formerly Swaziland),
uses craftsmanship and recycled glass to tell
folkloric tales in his work. In *The Chief Herdsman
and His Cattle*, he captures the tradition of
marriage by depicting a herd of cattle that is
a symbol of wealth and traditionally used as
payment between families when marital
agreements are made. — *SJJ*

KIRSTIE REA

Australia (b. 1955)

From a Still Point 1
and *From a Still Point 4*

Digital inkjet print on glass;
steel frame

Each: 100 x 52.5 x 6.5 cm

Photo: David Paterson

SJJ, BL, SJS

From a Still Point 1 and *4*
harness the intrinsic properties
of glass—reflection, refraction,
and transparency—to present
a liminal unknown space. Rea's
works capture the way panes
of glass arbitrarily divide and
overlap the images they reflect, amplifying this effect by
documenting it with a glass
lens. The viewer ultimately
encounters Rea's works on
what appear to be windows,
adding another, very fitting
layer of complexity.   *—BL*

CHIEMI WATANABE

Japan (b. 1989)

Koukanouzu

Glass, engraved, adhered, painted, cold-worked

6 x 53 x 53 cm

Courtesy of Kanazawa Utatsuyama Kogei Kobo

AC, SJJ, BL

The attention to detail in this piece is incredible. The engraving is masterfully executed with extreme precision and then encapsulated in colorless glass. The combination of the two pushes the material toward technical and aesthetic perfection.   *— SJJ*

IDA WIETH

Denmark (b. 1983)

Reach

Blown, fused, and slumped glass;
metal oxide, copper wire

Left: 25 x 43 x 24 cm
Right: 32 x 30 x 25 cm

SJJ

Craft, texture, movement, and evidence of
process define Wieth's pieces. They are built of
glass tubes that, when bound together and bent
over copper wire, become curious objects with
aesthetic strength. The wire is left behind to tell
a story of the process and thus becomes an
important part of the pieces.   —*SJJ*

TOOTS ZYNSKY
United States (b. 1951)

Smokey Comet Installation I

Corning Eagle XG glass, pulled
to stringer, latheworked with hydrogen
torches, slumped, assembled

33 x 102 x 137 cm

SJJ, BL, SJS

I'm drawn to these sculptural objects, in which
the technique is very recognizable as the work
of Zynsky. But the objects are completely different and new. The allusion to form and function
has been taken away, leaving us with objects
that refer to the body and show a sensuous
approach to glass and materiality.   — SJJ

:(infra)
structures

exposing
employing
documenting
hidden structures
words
tiles
cells

G. WILLIAM BELL

STINE BIDSTRUP

RONAN BOUROULLEC
ERWAN BOUROULLEC
for Iittala Inc.

STEFANO BULLO
MATTEO SILVERIO

KEERYONG CHOI

MATTHEW CURTIS

MATTHEW DAY PEREZ

DAVID DERKSEN
for Tre Product

MEL DOUGLAS

KARIN FORSLUND

HEATHER HANCOCK

SOOBIN JEON

HELEN LEE

AYA OKI

MOMOO OMURO

CHRISTINE TARKOWSKI

SYLVIE VANDENHOUCKE

NORWOOD VIVIANO

QIN WANG

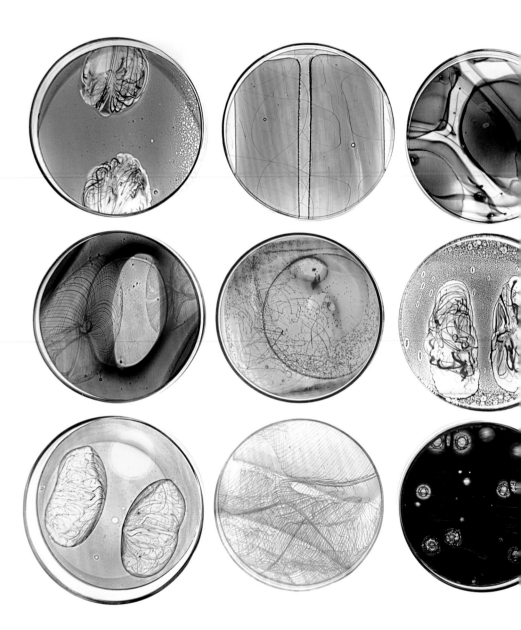

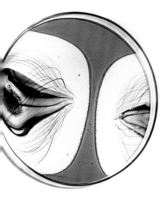

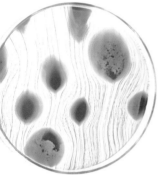

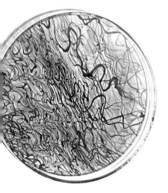

G. WILLIAM BELL

United Kingdom and United States
(b. 1985)

Abstract Thoughts

Blown and fused glass, cold-worked

10 x 64 x 45 cm

Photo: Annelie Grimwade Olofsson

AC, SJJ

For G. William Bell, glass is as much art as science. Experimenting with the formal and expressive possibilities of the material—whether blown, slumped, cut, or fused—he produces evocative patterns presented with laboratory-like precision. — AC

STINE BIDSTRUP
Denmark (b. 1982)

Bifurcation

Fused and stretched glass, cold-worked

56 x 15 x 15 cm

BL, SJS

Bifurcation reimagines and reinvents a traditional material—glass bangle bracelets—for a new purpose and a new audience. Fused, stretched, recombined, and cold-worked, the bangles retain their original pattern and coloration, but now allude to architecture, confectioners' constructions, and even the tangled computer cables that clutter junk drawers around the world.

Bidstrup embarked on this body of work following a residency at Anjali Srinivasan's ChoChoMa Studios in Chennai, India, which advocate the reinvigoration of traditional Indian crafts.   —SJS

RONAN BOUROULLEC
France (b. 1971)

and ERWAN BOUROULLEC
France (b. 1976)
for IITTALA INC. Finland

"Ruutu" Vases

Blown glass
Largest: 27.3 x 21 cm

AC, SJJ

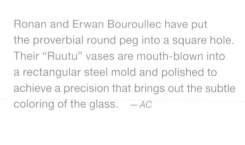

Ronan and Erwan Bouroullec have put the proverbial round peg into a square hole. Their "Ruutu" vases are mouth-blown into a rectangular steel mold and polished to achieve a precision that brings out the subtle coloring of the glass.   — *AC*

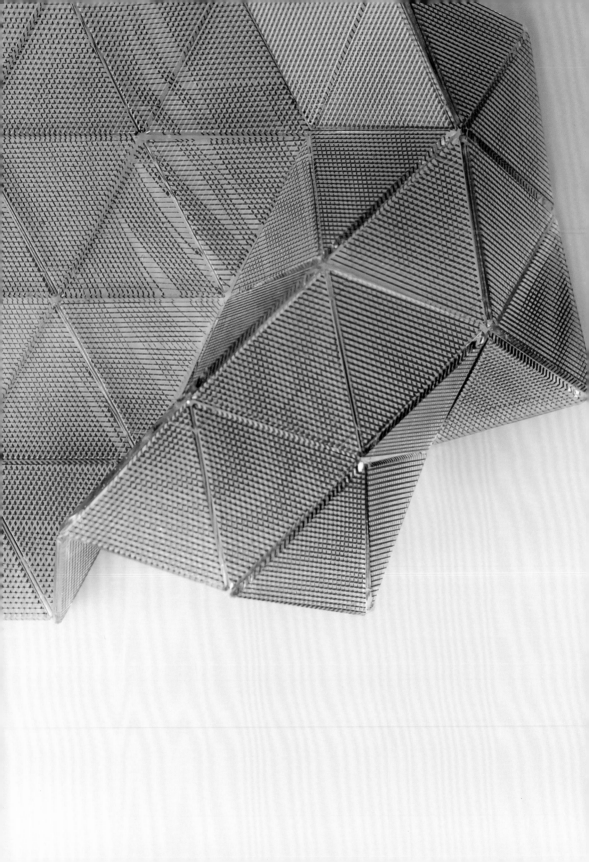

STEFANO BULLO
Italy (b. 1985)
and MATTEO SILVERIO
Italy (b. 1985)

Serapè

Fused glass; silkscreened vitreous enamel

32 x 55 x 0.8 cm

Photo: MAP/Murano Art Project

AC, SJJ, SJS

The Murano Art Project's *Serapè* is an innovative experiment with glass as an applied material. Inspired by 19th-century processes developed on Murano, triangular glass panels—hinged to create a flexible surface—are screenprinted with digitally generated filigree reed patterns that produce a parallax effect.   *— AC*

KEERYONG CHOI

United Kingdom (b. 1976)

Daam Dah

Kiln-formed glass; gold-leaf inlay

Tallest: 12 x 13.8 x 9.8 cm

AC, SJJ, BL, SJS

Tradition and perfection are what first come
to my mind when I look at these glass jars.
Choi has an ongoing inner negotiation between
herself and the medium of glass in order to
achieve the best possible and controlled result.
The lidded jars are a stunning result of these
efforts. They are perfect in their skilled craftsmanship and elegant shape, contemporary and
yet traditional.   *— SJJ*

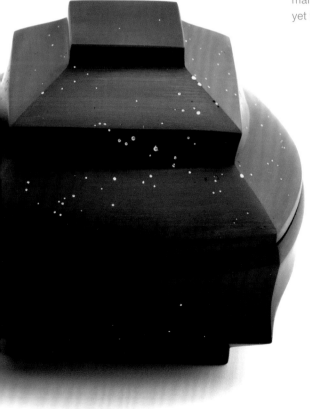

MATTHEW CURTIS
Australia (b. 1964)

Amber Increment

Cast tinted glass; stainless steel armature

50 x 170 x 50 cm

Photo: Rob Little

AC, BL

Matthew Curtis's *Amber Increment* is a striking architectural use of glass, with its cellular glass "lenses" articulating its parabolic form. — *AC*

MATTHEW DAY PEREZ

United States (b. 1984)

Grade

Fused and silvered glass, cold-worked

190 x 205 x 6 cm

Photo: Martyna Szczesna

SJJ

Day Perez is interested in how glass has the capacity to hold, react to, and shape light. In *Grade*, he has created wall objects that look like large, broken, and reassembled mirrors that become luminous wall installations. — *SJJ*

DAVID DERKSEN

The Netherlands (b. 1983)

for TRE PRODUCT Poland

"1L" Carafe and "0,2L" Glass

Latheworked laboratory borosilicate glass; screen-printed enamel

Left: 31.5 x 7.5 x 7.5 cm

Right: 6.3 x 7.5 x 7.5 cm

AC, SJJ, SJS

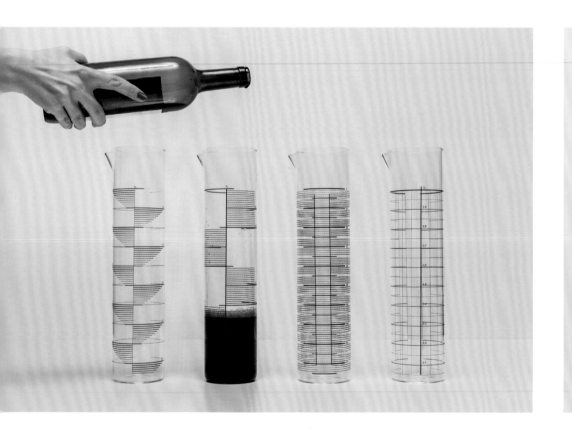

Designed for the Polish company Tre Product and fabricated in the Czech Republic, these pieces use the global language of science to create tableware that is eminently appealing and delightfully functional. I'm drawn to the way these pitchers and cups emphasize the aesthetic dimension of traditional labware; by increasing the number and arrangement of the measuring stripes, Derksen has created pieces that are both timeless and playful. — SJS

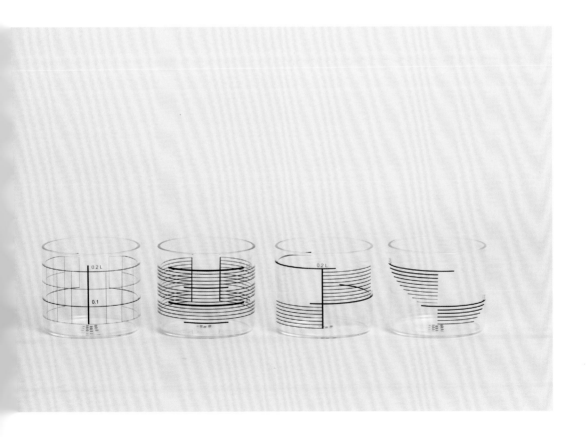

MEL DOUGLAS

Australia (b. 1978)

Borderline

Kiln-formed glass, cold-worked

94 x 139.7 x 2.5 cm

Photo: David Paterson

SJJ, BL, SJS

With its repetition of circles, *Borderline* could be depicting an optical response to physical space, such as the dilation and contraction of the pupil or the sun's disappearance and reappearance during an eclipse. However, what appears as line in Douglas's work is actually the result of carefully calculated sculptural fusing techniques. The result, which simultaneously holds the viewer's gaze on the surface and pushes it beyond, gives line a power beyond drawing; it is now a full actor in the construction of three-dimensional space. *— BL*

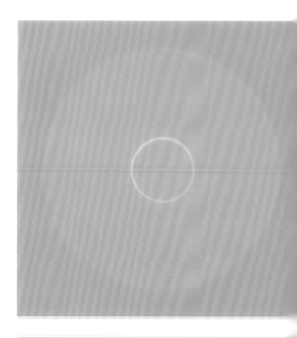

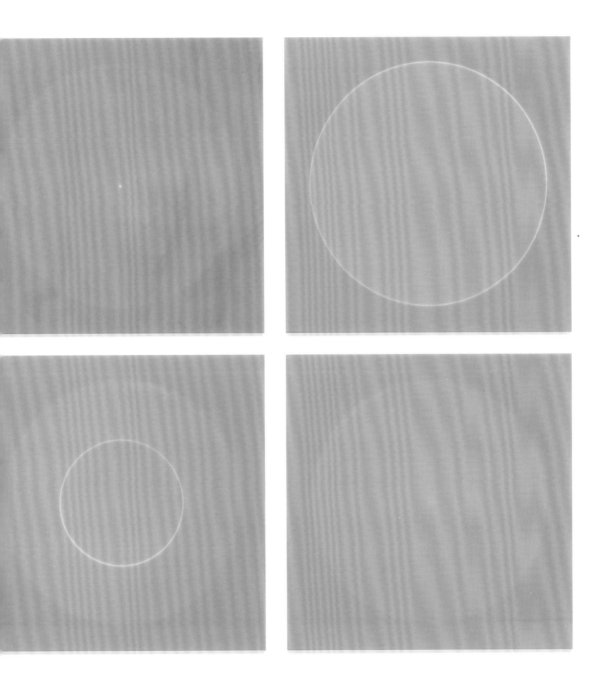

KARIN FORSLUND

Sweden and Norway (b. 1984)

Expanding Matter – Cylinder Series

Kiln-cast glass

Each: 30 x 35 x 20 cm

Photo: Russell Johnson

SJJ, BL, SJS

Forslund experiments with materiality and the language of crafts, and in doing so, she also questions the definition of the material we know as glass. By pushing the creative starting point back to before the combination of materials and chemistry becomes glass, she is able to create a new matter in which the firing process and the transformation of the matter define the final shape and become the narrative of the piece. — *SJJ*

HEATHER HANCOCK
Canada (b. 1969)

REFLECT 3.2 curve

Cut glass; grout

122 x 76.2 cm

AC, BL

Heather Hancock uses glass inlay to re-create
the geometries of Miesian architectural facades,
capturing a sense of the ephemeral within their
otherwise highly rational compositions.   — *AC*

SOOBIN JEON

Republic of Korea (b. 1991)

Terrazzo and Its Reinterpretation

Fused and blown glass

Dimensions vary

AC, BL, SJS

Inspired both by the composition of terrazzo
and by the view through the microscope lens,
Soobin Jeon's tableware features poetic
juxtapositions of color that both allude to and
seem to transcend their natural and built world
referents. Dots of red, dashes of green, slashes
of purple, and swaths of peach add punctuation
to this almost textual series of vessels.   —*SJS*

HELEN LEE

United States (b. 1978)

Alphabit

Murrine, low-iron float glass; stainless steel, aluminum, acrylic, LEDs

121.9 x 91.4 x 45.7 cm

Photo: Levi Mandel

SJJ, BL, SJS

In *Alphabit*, a glass cabinet for letterpress type, the visual artist and graphic designer Helen Lee explores the rematerialization of the written word in the computer age. Here, glass letters in five sizes replace the lead type of traditional letterpress. Produced in the ancient technique of *murrine*, which, like computer vector graphics, allows for easy resizing, and displayed in back-lighted trays reminiscent of device screens, Lee's letters foreground the role of glass in contemporary communication and, by extension, in the formation of contemporary thought.   —*SJS*

AYA OKI

Japan (b. 1982)

Fate

Blown glass

23 x 28 x 24 cm

Photo: Andrew Thompson

SJJ

Volume, restrained expansion, stretching, and magnification. Fascinated by the craftsmanship and properties of glass, Oki creates objects that harness the way the material changes when it is being transformed by glassblowing. The pattern of thin lines and the use of transparent, fading colors emphasize the notion of expansion and restraint in this beautiful piece. —*SJJ*

MOMOO OMURO

Japan (b. 1969)

vessel / black

Pâte de verre

18 x 23 x 23 cm

Photo: Keisuke Osumi

SJJ, SJS

There is something so appealing about the subtle symmetry and structure in Omuro's translucent *pâte de verre* vessel. Reminiscent of architecture and straddling the visual line between ceramics and glass, it has an allure and grace all its own.   —*SJS*

CHRISTINE TARKOWSKI

United States (b. 1967)

Copper Pour

Poured glass and poured copper;
copper mesh, steel

Dimensions vary

SJJ, BL, SJS

In *Copper Pour*, molten glass and copper
are employed to fret and conceal geometric
armatures. The resulting work choreographs
a moment in time: the repetition of process
expediting a disintegration of order.   — BL

SYLVIE VANDENHOUCKE

Belgium (b. 1969)

Converging Line II

Pâte de verre; aluminum frame

93 x 93 x 5 cm

Photo: MUTED ed.

SJJ, BL, SJS

Made through a repetitive drawing-like practice, *Converging Line II* demonstrates an affinity with the principles of abstraction. Subtle and with a self-determined logic, Vandenhoucke's works read like a latter-day Agnes Martin painting in which line, dashes, and stripes have been replaced by delicate, fingerprint-size *pâte de verre* castings.   — BL

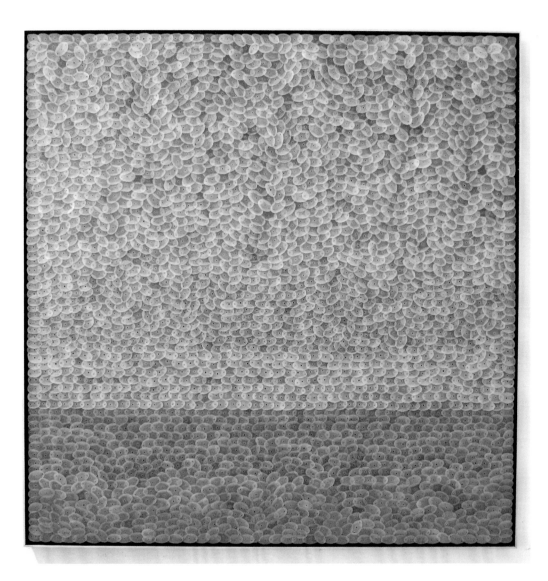

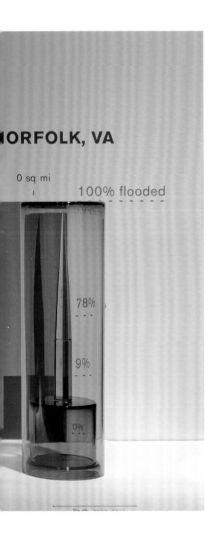

NORFOLK, VA

0 sq mi

100% flooded

78%

9%

0%

NORWOOD VIVIANO
United States (b. 1972)

Cities Underwater
(detail of *New Orleans, Newark, Norfolk*)

Blown glass; cut vinyl drawings; animation

Dimensions vary

Photo: Cathy Carver

AC, SJJ, BL, SJS

The magnitude of the effects of climate change can be hard to fathom. Through *Cities Underwater*, Norwood Viviano offers a clear visualization of what's at stake: nesting glass cylinders correlate with the amount of land that's projected to be lost in cities across the United States because of rising sea levels. *— AC*

NEW ORLEANS, LA

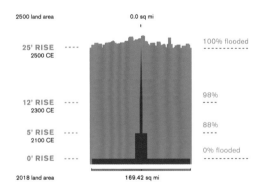

2500 land area

0.0 sq mi

100% flooded

25' RISE
2500 CE

98%

12' RISE
2300 CE

88%

5' RISE
2100 CE

0% flooded

0' RISE

2018 land area

169.42 sq mi

QIN WANG

China (b. 1978)

Tranquility–The Scholar's Four Treasures

Cast glass

Overall: 30 x 37 x 25 cm

AC, SJS

Qin Wang takes the "four treasures" of the classical Chinese study—the tools of Chinese calligraphy that denote a cultivated life—and unusually translates them into glass. As such, he gives them added layers of meaning in a culture in which materials are deeply embedded with metaphorical associations.   — AC

:body politic

present
tense critical
commentaries
glass
identity
surveillance
gender

TAMÁS ÁBEL

MONICA BONVICINI

DEBORAH CZERESKO

DORIS DARLING

ROSS DELANO
ERIKH VARGO
BRAD PATOCKA

ABDULNASSER GHAREM

FREDRIK NIELSEN

SUZANNE PECK
KAREN DONNELLAN

MEGAN STELLJES

MARK ZIRPEL

TAMÁS ÁBEL

Hungary (b. 1991)

Colour Therapy: Washington, D.C. + Budapest

Video, 2 min., 40 sec.

Photo: Terre Nguyen and Benedek Bognár

BL, SJS

Simple, direct, and beautiful, Tamás Ábel's
Colour Therapy is a powerful statement
of queer presence. In this performance, Ábel
used a fabricated glass mirror to reflect the
rainbow flag onto the Millennium Monument in
his hometown of Budapest, Hungary, and the
Washington Monument in Washington, D.C.,
bringing his subtle and resonant protest to
the spiritual heart of each nation.   *— SJS*

MONICA BONVICINI

Italy (b. 1965)

Bonded

Hot-worked glass; metal belt buckles

84 x 47 x 47 cm

Photo: Francesco Allegretto
and Berengo Studio

SJJ

Bonvicini explores themes such as sexuality, power, and gender in this provocative bundle of glass and metal. By rendering clothing accessories that refer to male dominance in the cold and inflexible material of glass, she emphasizes the emotional strength of the piece.   — *SJJ*

DEBORAH CZERESKO

United States (b. 1961)

Meat Chandelier

Blown glass; metal armature

244 x 152 x 152 cm

Photo: Jess Julius

BL

In this feminist send-up of traditional Venetian chandeliers, Czeresko replaces the form's typical flowered frills with impeccably sculpted cuts of meat, links of sausage, slices of prosciutto, and whole, dangling salamis. It is a humorous and whimsical take on the male-dominated and casually sexist arena of the hot shop, entirely in line with the aims of an artist who seeks to make work "that addresses feminist issues but is not isolationist."   *—BL*

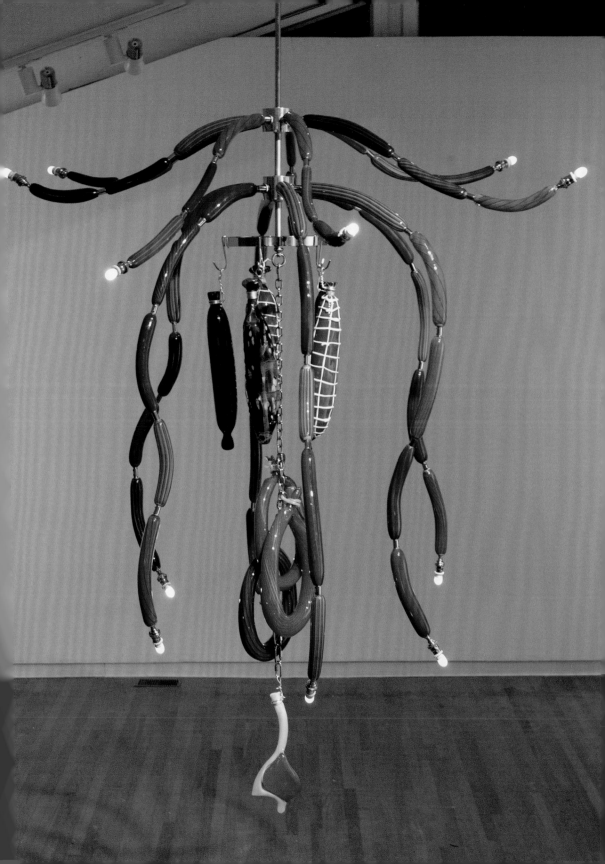

DORIS DARLING
Austria (b. 1980)

"Super Strong" Lamp
Blown glass; brass
30 x 130 x 30 cm
Photo: Klaus Pichler
AC, SJJ, BL, SJS

Glass and light are combined so well in this stylish, contemporary light source. I'm fascinated by how Darling offers a playful, humorous, and feminist statement about our attention to objects and how we stage ourselves and our surroundings, making our homes a personal statement.   *—SJJ*

ROSS DELANO
United States (b. 1986)

ERIKH VARGO
United States (b. 1990)

and BRAD PATOCKA
United States (b. 1990)

Le Pressepapier Executiv

Glass, rose petals, sweat, vision

Digital video, 4 min.

AC, BL

Le Pressepapier Executiv is a satirical melodrama that heightens the grave dilemma facing artists: life's impermanence and the romantic notion of transcendence through the making of objects. The parody highlights the narcissism and exhibitionism on display within the hot shop and sacrifices plenty of flowers in the process.   —BL

What do we leave behind?

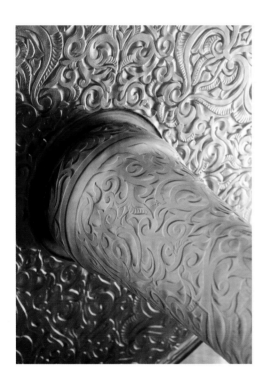

ABDULNASSER GHAREM
Saudi Arabia (b. 1973)

The Stamp (Moujaz)

Blown glass; handmade engraving

120 x 90 x 90 cm

Photo: Francesco Allegretto
and Berengo Studio

AC, SJJ, BL

The Stamp (Moujaz) features the word *moujaz* (permitted) in the center, surrounded by the phrase "In accordance with Sharia law" in English and Arabic. The monumental scale of this official tool calls into question the roles in which cultural, governmental, and theological constructs define the body politic. —*BL*

FREDRIK NIELSEN

Sweden (b. 1977)

I was here

Mixed media

Installation

Photo: Courtesy of Dunkers Kulturhus

AC, SJJ, BL, SJS

Covered in hot-pink graffiti proclaiming the
artist's phone number and full of thick, oversized glass vessels hidden under a glittery
coating of automotive paint, Fredrik Nielsen's
installations are easy to read as self-aggrandizing
expressions of macho potency. But to read
them that way is to miss the point because,
beneath this subversive exterior, Nielsen's
pieces are actually an assertion of presence
for Swedish glassworking, full of reverence for
its long history and trepidation at the rapidly
disappearing jobs for its factory gaffers. *— SJS*

Alternative Lexicons for the Hotshop

Neutral

Gloryhole	Reheating chamber
Jacks	Splinchers, vertical constrictors
Blow partner	Glass partner, assistant
Gaffer	Leader
Strip off	Peel
Flash	Maintain, babysit
Blow	Give me air, puff, on/off
Suck	Inhale, sip
Jacking	Constricting
Moile	Anchor
Marver slut/tart	Young person eager to learn

Feminist

Gloryhole	G spot
Jacks	Jills, janes
Blow partner	Doula
Gaffer	Gamma
Strip off	Chippendale
Jack and crack	Flicking the bean
Open the lip	Dilate
Get 'er hot	Get 'er hot
Shearing	Scissoring
Jacking	Kegels, straddling
Popping a bubble	Crowning
Furnace	Uterus
Tweezers	Tweez-hers

High Brow

Gloryhole	The chamber of the glorious corona of life affirming heat
Jacks	Exalted irons of constriction
Blow partner	Minion, companion in fire
Gaffer	Her royal majesty
Strip off	Whisk away excessive layers
Flash	Momentarily return to the blaze from whence you came
Blow	Exhale with vigor
Suck	Inhale with vigor
Moile	Foundation of the architecture of my creation
Popping a bubble	The emergence of all possibilities

Expanded

_____
_____
_____
_____
_____
_____
_____
_____

Exhalewithvigor.org   Karen Donnellan and Suzanne Peck, 2018

SUZANNE PECK
United States (b. 1980)

and KAREN DONNELLAN
Republic of Ireland (b. 1986)

Blow Harder: Alternative Lexicons for the Hotshop

Social practice, etymology, language, inkjet print on paper

91.4 x 61 cm

AC, BL, SJS

Blow Harder: Alternative Lexicons for the Hotshop is an etymological analysis of the sexually charged language of American glassblowing. It deftly critiques the historically male-dominated hot shop by analyzing the vocabulary that has sprung from it. Peck and Donnellan's proposal for alternative terms calls for a reckoning with the power dynamics, safety, and inclusivity of the glassblowing process.   — *BL*

MEGAN STELLJES

United States (b. 1987)

This Shit is Bananas

Sculpted glass; neon

76.2 x 45.7 x 10.2 cm

Photo: Alec Miller

SJS

Harnessing the humor that has been part of
artistic glassworking since the Funky 1960s,
Stelljes's piece is a funny, witty, and astute
political commentary. Oh, and those bananas?
Hot-sculpted glass. Impressive.   —*SJS*

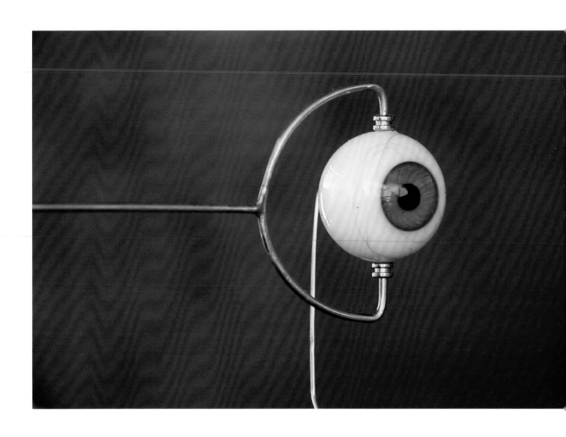

MARK ZIRPEL

United States (b. 1956)

Observer

Flameworked glass; steel, magnets, motor

82.6 x 43.2 x 43.2 cm

AC, SJJ, BL, SJS

A robotic glass eyeball that appears to follow its viewers, *Observer* is an Orwellian automaton, surveilling viewers as they gaze upon it. Humorous but sinister, the piece comments on the governmental gaze, taking on even greater resonance in our time of heightened tribalism and anxiety. — *BL*

:embodied knowledge

made with
about
in absence of
the body

KATE BAKER

DYLAN BRAMS

NADÈGE DESGENÉTEZ

JAHDAY FORD
JOSEPH HILLARY

JOCHEN HOLZ

KRISTA ISRAEL
Ayako Tani
Hans de Kruijk

MICHA KARLSLUND

JENNIFER KEMARRE
MARTINIELLO

JITKA KOLBE-RŮŽIČKOVÁ

DANNY LANE

SHAYNA LEIB

GEOFFREY MANN

ZORA PALOVÁ
ŠTĚPÁN PALA

LAURA PUSKA

AUSTIN STERN

C. MATTHEW SZÖSZ

BLANCHE TILDEN

CECILIA UNTARIO

DUSTIN YELLIN

HE ZHAO

KATE BAKER

Australia (b. 1973)

Within Matter #2

UV flatbed digitally printed glass;
raw steel

105 x 120 x 95 cm

SJJ, SJS

Kate Baker's photographic assemblages
challenge what I think I know about material, the
body, and movement. Her paradoxical approach
to convention—the way she creates a portrait
with no face, on glass whose "glassiness" has
been subsumed by a representation of metal—
invests her piece with an incredible allure.
It is compelling work that implores me to keep
looking, to keep trying to understand what is
just beyond my grasp.   *— SJS*

DYLAN BRAMS
United States and Israel (b. 1979)

039 to 058

Photograph

Photo: Lena Dubinsky

AC, SJJ, BL, SJS

For 15 years, Dylan Brams has used the Venetian *ampolina* form as a test of his glassblowing skills, similar to the way a pianist might practice scales. *039 to 058* records 19 of those attempts as a layered, digital composite photograph. I'm drawn to the way this project both glorifies making and eradicates the individual object. —BL

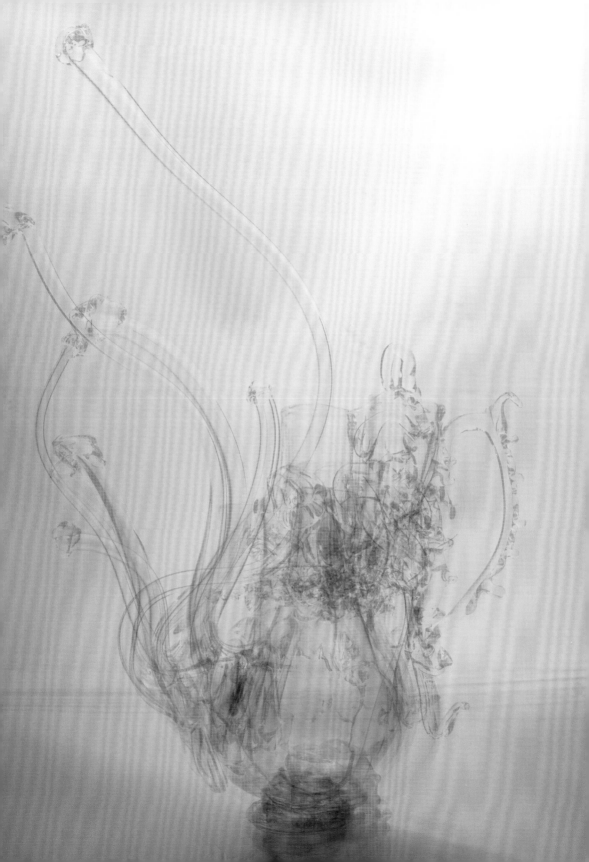

NADÈGE DESGENÉTEZ

France and United States (b. 1973)

Promise

Blown and sculpted glass, mirrored, carved, hand-sanded; wood

146 x 95 x 76 cm

Photo: Greg Piper

SJJ, BL, SJS

With references to the body, Desgenétez creates large blown sculptures that are both sensuous and strong. Their impressive appearance in scale and skill is underlined only when she mirrors them, in combination with the graduated use of color and soft surface treatment. — *SJJ*

JAHDAY FORD
Bermuda (b. 1994)

and JOSEPH HILLARY
United Kingdom (b. 1994)

Breathe

Glass blown into CNC carved mold, cut

28 x 9 x 25 cm

Photo: Ester Segarra

AC, SJS

Deriving its shape from the sound waves
generated from blowing glass, the *Breathe*
vase conflates maker, making, and object
in a single gesture. — *AC*

JOCHEN HOLZ

Germany (b. 1970)

"Penguin" Jugs

Lampworked colored borosilicate glass

24 x 16 x 12 cm

Photo: Angus Mill

AC, SJJ, BL, SJS

There's something so personable about Holz's
playful "Penguin" jugs. Delightfully round and
misshapen, they are formed in the image of the
body and with the hands of the user in mind.
They are colorful, confidently tactile reminders
that perfection can take many forms.   — *SJS*

KRISTA ISRAEL
The Netherlands (b. 1975)

AYAKO TANI (research)
Japan and United Kingdom (b. 1981)
and HANS DE KRUIJK (research)
The Netherlands (b. 1947)

Lapi Boli Project and **Pâte de verre**
Vases in the Lapi Boli *Technique*

Video, 4 min.

Largest: 7 x 5.5 x 5.5 cm

Project assistants: Hao Ran Zhu,
Wilma Hornsveld

Photo: Liu Peng

AC, SJJ, BL, SJS

From time to time, a new development just hits
you, and all of a sudden, you can't see the world
in the same way again. That's how I feel about
the *Lapi Boli Project*, a far-ranging enterprise
bringing together artists and artisans from four
countries for the incredibly innovative task of
throwing *pâte de verre* on the pottery wheel. Such
a simple idea and such incredible impact.   — SJS

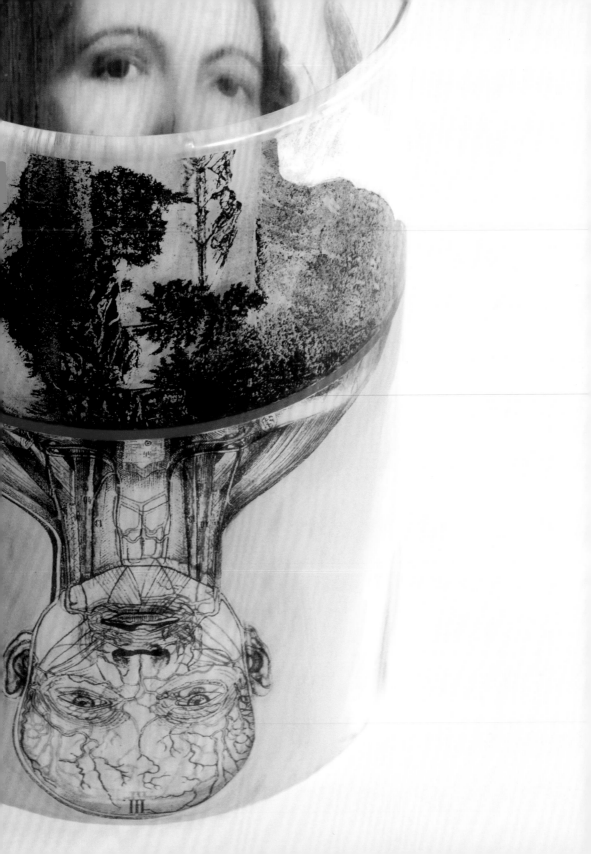

MICHA KARLSLUND
Denmark (b. 1963)

Sibylla with X

Blown glass; decals, enamel,
sandblasted details

24 x 16 x 16 cm

AC, SJJ

In this cylindrical jar, Karlslund combines her
glassmaking skills and her background as a
visual artist. The blown glass cylinder becomes
the canvas for personal narrative collages with
rendered images that originate from her paintings,
drawings, and photographs. The transparency
of glass is used to reveal and layer segments
of images in what becomes three-dimensional
collages.   *—SJJ*

JENNIFER KEMARRE MARTINIELLO

Australia [Arrernte] (b. 1949)

Red Sedge Reeds Fish Basket

Blown glass, cold-worked

29 x 59 x 35 cm

Photo: Art Atelier

AC, SJJ, BL

Jennifer Kemarre Martiniello draws from the traditional weaving work of her Australian Aboriginal heritage to create glass vessels that elegantly abstract the former's interplay of light, form, and line.   *— AC*

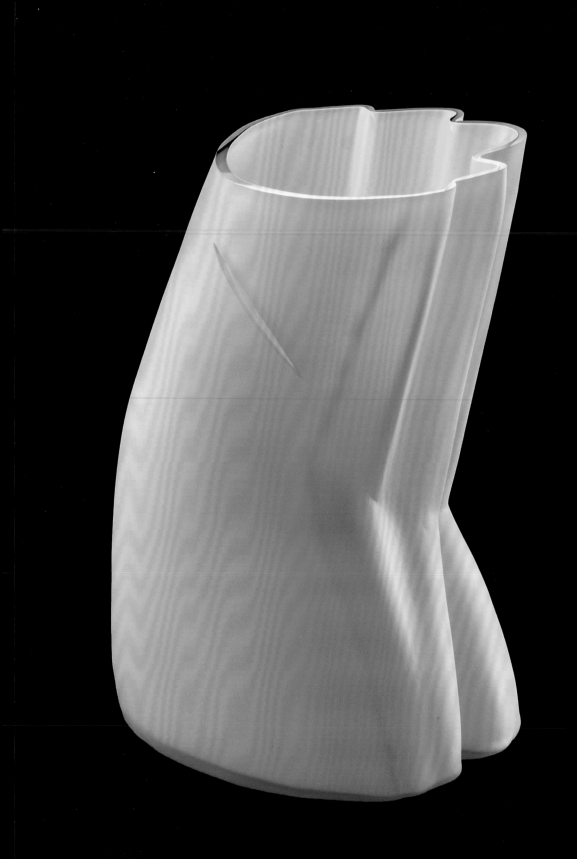

JITKA KOLBE-RŮŽIČKOVÁ

Czech Republic (b. 1959)

Gerda Stein

Glass blown in a gypsum mold, cut, sandblasted

45 x 38 x 32 cm

Photo: Gabriel Urbánek

SJJ, BL

A piece made in witness to the continued reverberations of the Holocaust, *Gerda Stein* records the absence of its namesake. Sent to a Nazi concentration camp, Stein was first dehumanized—her hair shorn, her soft dress replaced by the scratchy fabric of a prisoner's garb—and eventually murdered. By translating her lost dress into a glass vessel—star-yellow and slashed, as if in ritual mourning—Kolbe-Růžičková has memorialized Stein's humanity and pointed to the incalculable impact of so many extinguished lives.   — *BL*

DANNY LANE

United States (b. 1955)

Carved Cast 1

Float glass cast in carved plaster
with controlled devitrification

92 x 92 x 11 cm

Photo: Peter Wood

BL

Lane employed an intimate knowledge of glass
process to imagine and realize *Carved Cast 1*.
The resulting work conjures ancient Greek relief
sculpture, its narrative possibly lost to erosion
or time.   *— BL*

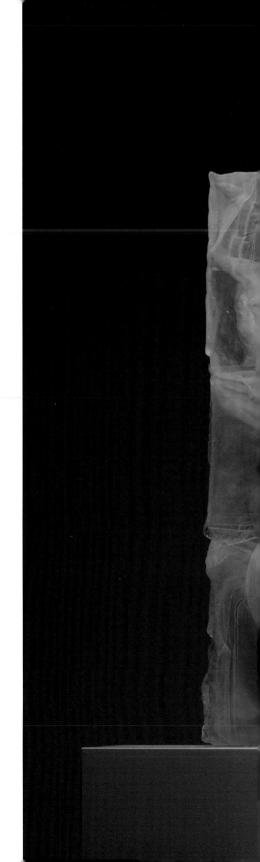

SHAYNA LEIB

United States (b. 1975)

Gâteau au fromage et chocolat,
Gâteau au fromage et la framboise,
and *Tarte aux mûres* (from the series
"Patisserie")

Lampworked glass; thrown ceramic

Largest: 10.2 x 10.2 x 9.5 cm

Photo: Eric Tadsen

AC, SJJ

Society has a lot to say about what, how much, and when we eat. Leib makes pastries in glass as part of her own therapeutic process about food. She creates perfect reproductions of pastry, in which the original function of eating is taken away, and what is left behind is a critical comment on society's view on the matter, ranging from joy and luxury to guilt. *— SJJ*

133

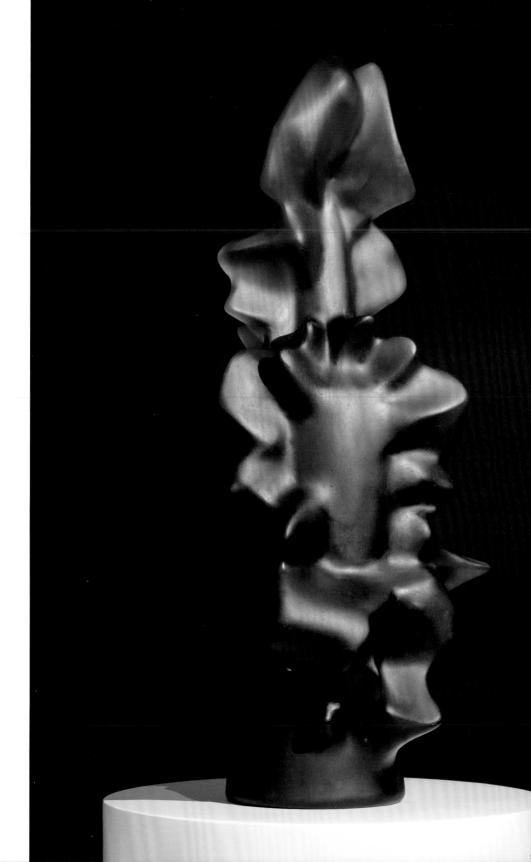

GEOFFREY MANN
United Kingdom (b. 1980)

The Leith Pattern, Mary

Kiln-cast glass; animation, 1 min., 45 sec.

35 x 15 x 10 cm

Photo: © National Museums Scotland

AC, SJS

Geoffrey Mann literally puts a message in a
wine bottle, making it an artifact of memory.
The form of his distorted, 3-D-printed bottle
is derived from audio recordings of residents
of Leith, Scotland—a once-thriving industrial
center where, according to local legend, that
vessel type was invented.   —AC

ZORA PALOVÁ
Slovakia (b. 1947)
and ŠTĚPÁN PALA
Czech Republic and Slovakia (b. 1944)

Fission

Mold-melted glass, cut, cold-worked

60 x 100 x 100 cm

Photo: Valeria Zacharova

AC, SJJ, BL

Imposing and contemplative, *Fission* is a
reflection on the life stage of motherhood,
synchronous in form yet cleaving apart. The
voids and hollow passes bring light to the
center of a piece that is otherwise massive,
with the density and material treatment of
abraded stone.   *—BL*

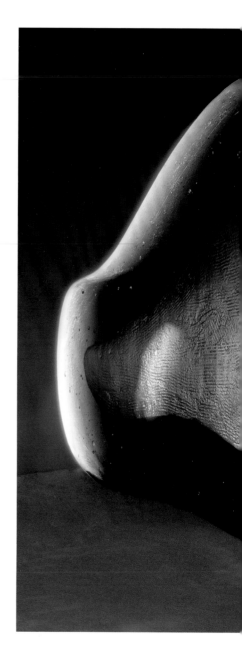

LAURA PUSKA

Finland (b. 1986)

Dialogue and a series of moments

Video, 29 min.

AC, SJJ, BL

Gestures represent a voice, and these gestures—mediated through the tool of glass—have become the main vocabulary in this wordless dialogue documented in Puska's video piece. The theme and content seem appropriate for the geographical point of departure for Puska's video work. As a viewer who does not understand the spoken language in the video, I'm reminded of the Finnish word *sisu*, which describes a special courage, determination, and silent communication that is found only in the northernmost part of the hemisphere, more precisely in Finland.   — *SJJ*

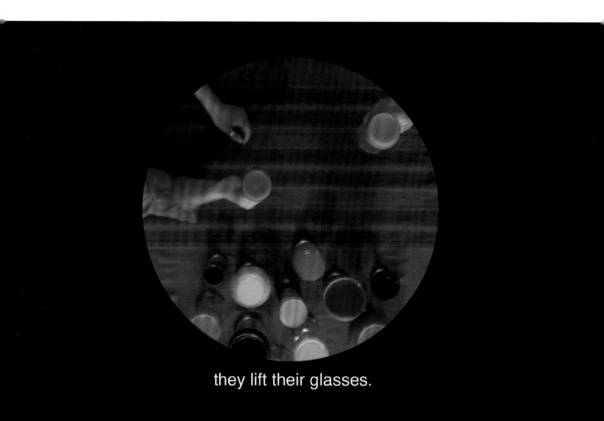

they lift their glasses.

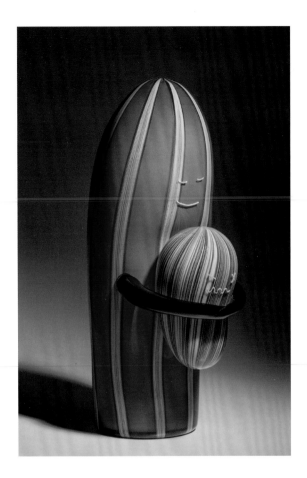

AUSTIN STERN

United States (b. 1989)

Hugged to Death, Creeps,
and *All Wound Up*
(from the series "Little Monsters")

Blown and hot-sculpted glass

Largest: 56 x 26 x 23 cm

Photo: Alec Miller Arts

AC, SJJ, SJS

Playful and masterfully made, Stern's pieces perfectly encapsulate the current state of American glassblowing. His work excellently combines complex Venetian glassblowing techniques with the raucous humor of early Funk art–infused studio glass. — *SJS*

C. MATTHEW SZÖSZ

United States (b. 1974)

Reservoir

Woven and fused glass

40 x 40 x 35 cm

SJJ, SJS

A student of glass possibilities, Szösz takes novel approaches to glassforming in his work. For instance, to make the delicate, knotted structure of *Reservoir*, he first spun glass fiber into rope using a 19th-century ropemaking machine, wove it into its present form, and fired it over a refractory core. The result is something delicate and light, which scratches the itch of any glass enthusiast eager to see the material stretched to its technical and aesthetic limits.   — SJS

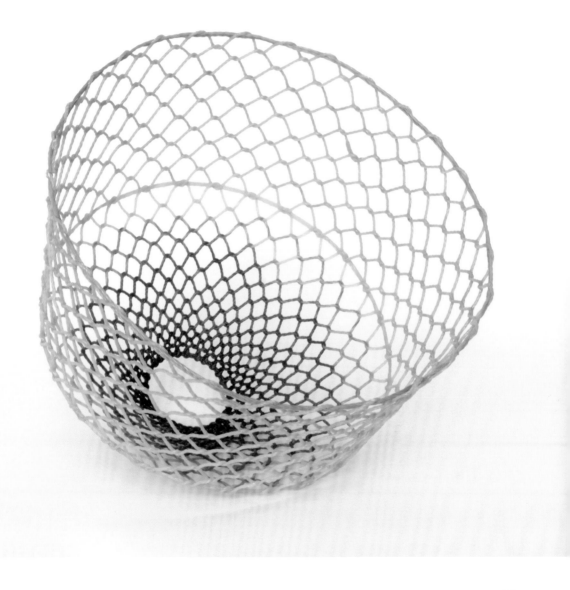

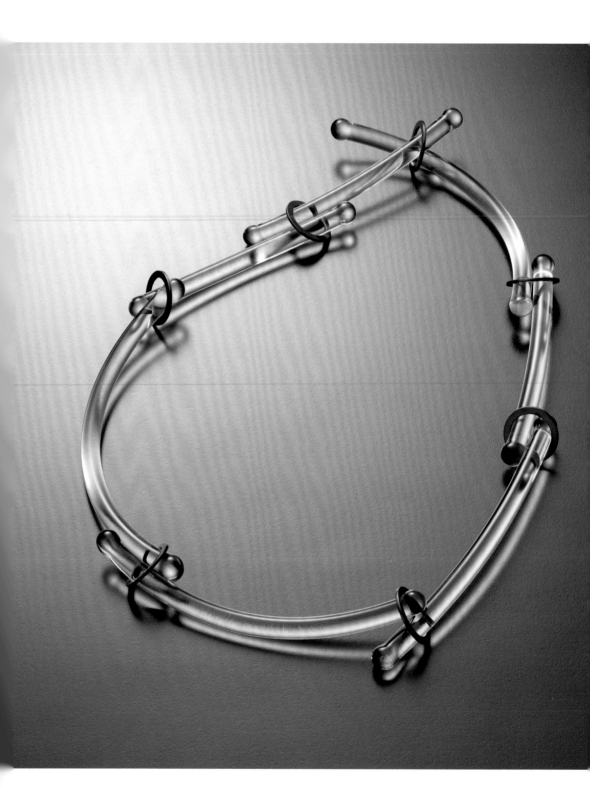

BLANCHE TILDEN

Australia (b. 1968)

"Flow" Necklace

Kiln-worked and flameworked
borosilicate glass; titanium

2 x 17 x 17 cm

Photo: Grant Hancock

SJS

I see "Flow" as a play on both the smooth,
almost waterlike fluidity of this necklace as it
moves across the wearer's chest and the deeply
engaging practice of flameworking. Hands on
glass rods, rods in the flame: flameworking is an
inducement to the *flow* state, relieving distraction
and focusing its practitioner only on the con-
stant present tense of molten glass.   *— SJS*

CECILIA UNTARIO

Indonesia (b. 1984)

Grandma

Lampworked borosilicate glass;
projector, UV glue

45 x 40 x 25 cm

AC, SJJ, BL, SJS

Placed on a projector like yesterday's math
homework, Untario's projected teapots could
be a didactic exposition excerpted straight from
Christopher Dresser's *Principles of Decorative
Design*. Form, design, technique, taste. Which
one do we study today?   — *SJS*

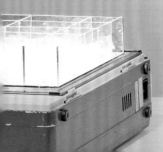

DUSTIN YELLIN

United States (b. 1975)

Cephaloproteus Riverhead (Four Hearts, Ten Brains, Blue Blood Drained through an Alembic)

Collage and acrylic on glass

180.7 x 68.6 x 40 cm

SJJ, BL, SJS

The drama in this piece is alluring. In this theater of nature, Yellin encapsulates the perilous inter-face between the natural world and the man-made one: the "great chain of being" is frozen in motion in an aquarium-like 3-D painting as it circulates through a body constructed of collaged images of skyscrapers. Here, we can anticipate the continuing disaster of climate change, but it is out of our reach. — SJJ

HE ZHAO

China (b. 1993)

You never notice

Lampworked glass; interactive infrared
sensor, motorized membrane

118 x 60 x 60 cm

AC, SJJ

With its sensor-activated, one-way mirrors
and kinetic, respirating membrane constantly
shifting the glass bubbles above it, He Zhao's
work is a poetic, interactive meditation on
breathing, fragility, and one's relationship with
the self.   *— AC*

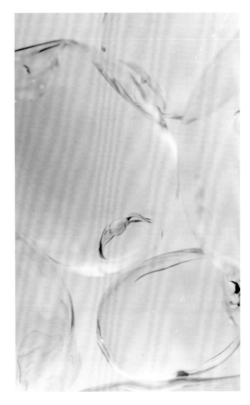

:01100111
01101100
01110011

post internet
recycled
recombinant
viral
digital
bright

JAMES AKERS

FLAVIE AUDI

JULI BOLAÑOS-DURMAN

DAVID COLTON

JUDI ELLIOTT

RAYMON ELOZUA

FRIDA FJELLMAN

DAVID KING

PEADAR LAMB

STANISLAV MULLER
RADKA MULLEROVA

SHARYN O'MARA

NATE RICCIUTO

TOMO SAKAI

ANGELA THWAITES

ERWIN WURM

JAMES AKERS

United States (b. 1993)

The Wild One (B)

Neon, circuit-bent toys, custom circuitry

61 x 97 x 69 cm

AC, SJS

James Akers makes systems out of whack. His
unruly assemblages of neon lights and hacked,
circuit-bent toys create glitchy feedback loops—
a kind of dissonant sensorial overload that is
perfectly in tune with our times. — *AC*

FLAVIE AUDI

France (b. 1986)

LCD (Lithic Crystalline Deposit) 5

Kiln-formed glass; aluminum

50 x 50 x 3.5 cm

Photo: Benjamin Westoby

BL, SJS

LCD (Lithic Crystalline Deposit) 5 employs glass's exceptional mutability to bridge the physical and virtual worlds. Recalling the sublime surface of an oil or chemical spill, the piece exudes a toxic, mystifying beauty, perhaps creating the conditions out of which a new utopian material future may arise. — BL

JULI BOLAÑOS-DURMAN

Costa Rica (b. 1984)

Two in One Goddess Headdress,
Tadpole Headdress, and *Fall Headdress*
(from the series "Made-Up Museum of Artefacts")

Blown and found glass, cut

Largest: 41 x 23 x 23 cm

Photo: Shannon Tofts

SJS

I'm attracted to the way these pieces celebrate the playfulness of the creative process. Bolaños-Durman's witty, friendly juxtapositions of found, purpose-made, and cast-off glass components are full of character, which she enhances through thoughtful cutting and carving. These headdresses, excerpted from the "Made-Up Museum of Artefacts" series, draw inspiration from historical heritage objects, but have been heavily filtered through the artist's improvisational, intuitive practice.   —SJS

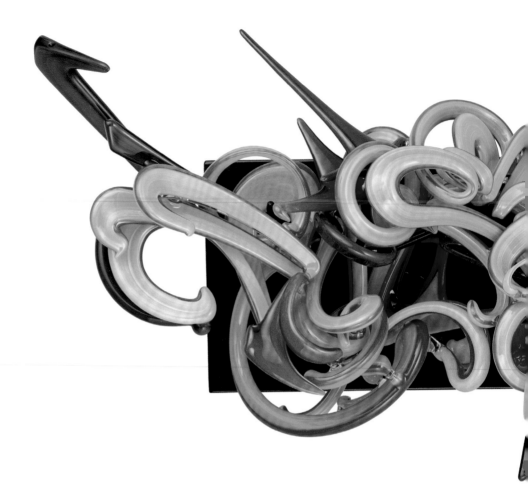

DAVID COLTON

United States (b. 1974)

Untitled, Corning Museum

Flameworked borosilicate glass; steel

30.5 x 66 x 23.5 cm

AC, SJJ, SJS

Inventive in material and technique, with broad popular appeal, glass marijuana pipes are one of the most important areas of glass production in the 21st century. Pipemakers, operating in a field that began before marijuana was legal in any constituency, often concealed the function of their pieces and, reviled by more mainstream artists and art movements, looked to street art for inspiration. Colton's expressive, abstract pipe, with its graffiti-like form and nearly hidden function, beautifully demonstrates the aesthetic influences and possibilities of this art form.   *— SJS*

JUDI ELLIOTT

Australia (b. 1934)

Architecture in the Environment 2

Kiln-formed glass

7 x 61 x 61 cm

Photo: Rob Little

SJJ, BL, SJS

Firmly rooted in a recognizable use of kiln forming, *Architecture in the Environment 2* defines a fresh, unexpected space. The tension between surface and depth, silhouette and mass, is masterfully rendered in a painterly, domestic-scale object.   — BL

RAYMON ELOZUA

United States (b. 1947)

R & D VII

Blown glass; welded steel rod; 04 terra-cotta
ceramic and glaze

109.2 x 58.4 x 96.5 cm

Glass fabricator: Lorin Silverman

AC, SJJ, BL

R & D VII exudes a raw, frenetic energy.
This assemblage of ceramic, glass, and
steel engages formal concerns addressed
in American Modernism, using the unique
qualities of each material to contrast form,
line, volume, and density.   *— BL*

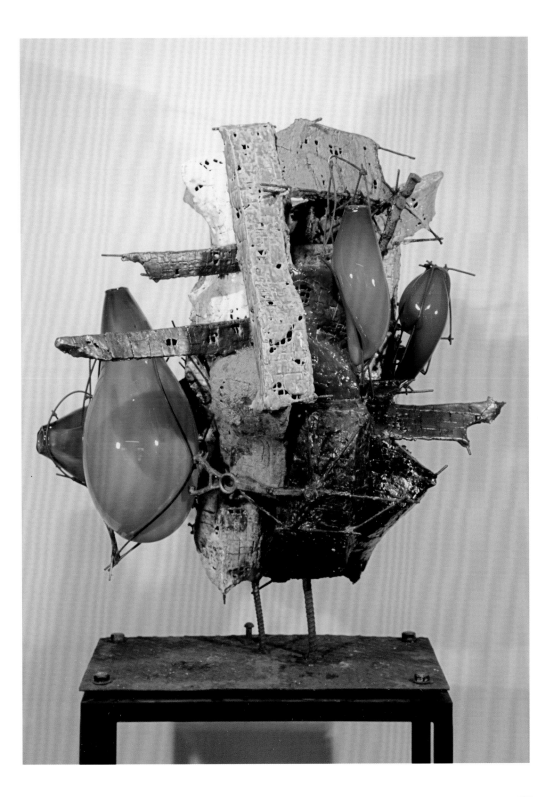

FRIDA FJELLMAN

Sweden (b. 1971)

Lustre Gothique Aux Saphirs

Blown glass; brass

203 x 101 x 101 cm

Photo: Robert J. Levin

SJJ, BL, SJS

Fjellman's innovative reinterpretation of the classic chandelier has resulted in this luxurious installation of suspended, oversized glass prisms laced into one another by drooping chains. It ought to create a spectacular statement and dramatic centerpiece to any space.   *— SJJ*

DAVID KING

United States (b. 1982)

Echo

Float glass, silicone, plastic

Largest: 10.2 x 15.2 x 12.7 cm

Photo: John Carlano

AC, BL, SJS

Echo takes glass into the realm of postindustrial Dada. Bits of found plastic are encased like relics in vitrine-like glass, posing questions about the relationship between the precious and the mundane, and the values we ascribe to scarcity. — *AC*

PEADAR LAMB
Republic of Ireland (b. 1966)

Yellow Form

Stained and painted glass

53 x 53 x 8 cm

Photo: Roland Paschhoff

SJJ, BL

Lamb's illuminated stained glass panel *Yellow Form* is a contemporary take on Celtic knotting. I also see references to calligraphy, hieroglyphs, and even—in its vibrating, roving line—the works of the painter Brice Marden.   *— BL*

STANISLAV MULLER
Czech Republic (b. 1971)

and RADKA MULLEROVA
Czech Republic (b. 1974)

Mirror Man on TV

Performance documentation

BL, SJS

The Mirror Man of *Mirror Man on TV* intervenes in his environment, inserting himself into the refuse of the 21st century with a potentially obsolete set of skills. Like a modern-day Norman Wilkinson, Muller and Mullerova brilliantly use mirror as razzle-dazzle camouflage to obscure where Mirror Man begins and ends, a fitting metaphor for the awkward transition into the digital age.   *— BL*

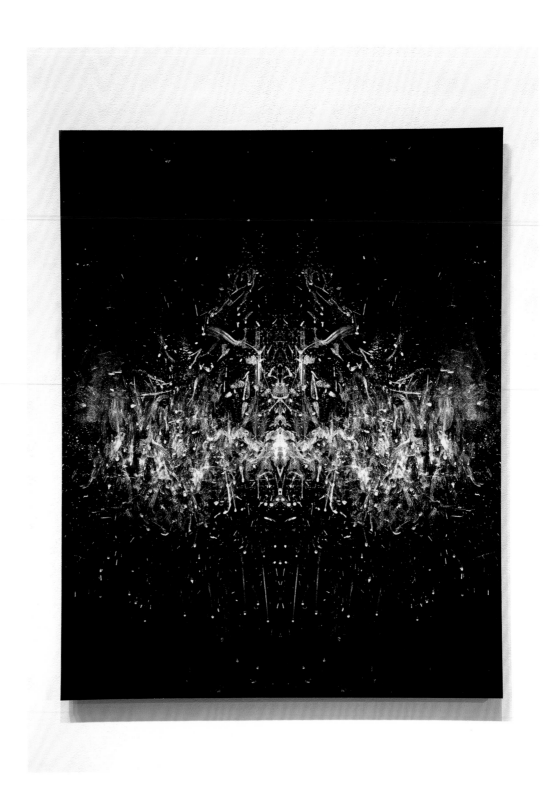

SHARYN O'MARA

United States (b. 1966)

Chandelier for the End of Time

Canine noseprints on glass; digital photograph
printed on metallic paper

95.3 x 76.2 x 2.5 cm

Photo: Defining Studios, Hartford, Connecticut

SJJ, BL

In *Chandelier for the End of Time*, the human
hand is sublimated to the non-human—in this
case, the canine nose. O'Mara's print is
determined solely by her dogs' movements on
glass, documented by photography and printed
on metallic paper. In this decidedly non-
anthropogenic work, the viewer is reminded
to pay attention to the rhythms, movements,
and mark-making happening around, because
of, or in spite of humans.   — BL

NATE RICCIUTO

United States (b. 1984)

Rise Over Run Again

Mirror, wood, cast glass, painted carpet, lights, fabricated steel, aluminum cans, acrylic, mixed media

275 x 340 x 250 cm

Photo: Tony Walsh

BL, SJS

In architecture, rise over run is used to calculate the height and depth of stairs and the slope of roofs. It is also a mathematical equation for determining the rate of change. In *Rise Over Run Again*, Ricciuto blends all of these ideas to chart the creative process, which is fantastical, intuitive, and unending. The piece creates a liminal, phantasmagoric space that blends the technological with the handmade, the traditional with the futuristic, the familiar with the imagined.   *— BL*

TOMO SAKAI

Japan (b. 1978)

Sunflowers and *Running Greyhound*

Glass sand, stop-motion animation video,
each: 15 sec.

BL, SJS

Occasionally, the most direct processes reveal
the best results. This is the case with *Sunflowers*
and *Running Greyhound*, compelling narrative
animations created with loose glass frit and the
immediacy of the iPhone.　　—BL

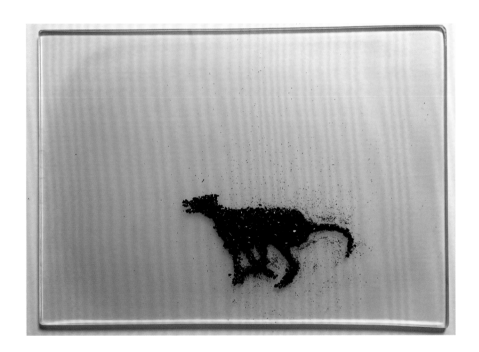

ANGELA THWAITES

United Kingdom (b. 1960)

Vessel Line-Up

Kiln-cast glass from 3-D-printed model

Largest: 8 x 7 x 3.5 cm

Photo: Dave Lawson

AC, BL

To create these vessels, Angela Thwaites
digitally models and 3-D prints their forms
before making molds and casting them in
glass. That is to say, the design is 3-D-printed
but, despite appearances, the final object isn't.
That makes this a fascinating, transitional work
that exists between the technical limits of a
new(ish) fabrication technology and its hold
on our imagination.   *— AC*

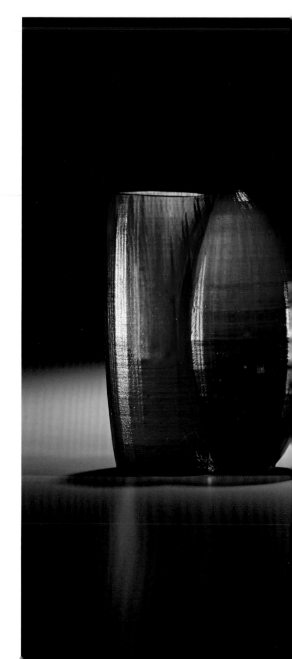

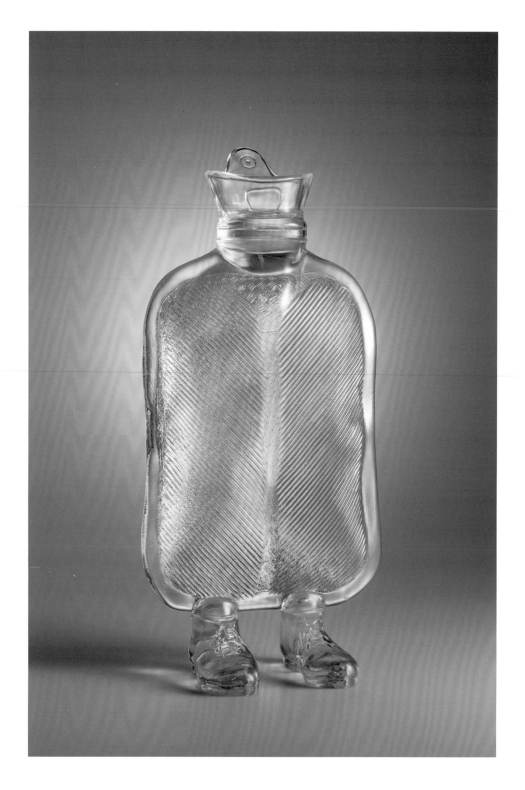

ERWIN WURM

Austria (b. 1954)

Mutter

Injection-cast glass

38 x 19 x 6 cm

Photo: Francesco Allegretto
and Berengo Studio

AC, BL

The artist Erwin Wurm has long questioned
definitions of sculpture with humorous,
sometimes absurd works, using everyday
objects placed in unexpected situations or
juxtapositions. Made on Murano, *Mutter*—
a hot-water bottle on legs—is no exception,
offering a different take on glass figurines.   *— AC*

:phenomena

im/material
wonder
transformative
experience
break
pop
shine

TORD BOONTJE
for Swarovski

LOTHAR BÖTTCHER

SHAUN CONROY

ALICIA EGGERT

MARIA BANG ESPERSEN

NICKOLAUS FRUIN

MARTINO GAMPER
for J. & L. Lobmeyr

KATHERINE GRAY

JIRO KAMATA

KARINA MALLING

AMIE McNEEL

SEAN MERCHANT

LUKAS MILANAK

MICHAL MOTYCKA

AARON PEXA

TOMÁŠ PROKOP

ANNA RILEY

JEROEN VERHOEVEN
JOEP VERHOEVEN

BOHYUN YOON

TORD BOONTJE

The Netherlands (b. 1968)
for SWAROVSKI Austria

"Radiant Light" Wall Light

Injection-molded lead-free crystal; brass, LEDs

6.8 x 18 x 18 cm

AC, SJS

Tord Boontje's "Radiant Light" rethinks the
refractive possibilities of crystals. Boontje
worked with Swarovski to develop three
new crystal shapes that are organic, rather
than faceted, to produce light that ripples
on the wall.   *—AC*

LOTHAR BÖTTCHER

Republic of South Africa
and Germany (b. 1973)

Pocket Lens

Hand-cut optical glass, polished

14.5 x 7 x 1.5 cm

AC, SJJ, BL, SJS

Call me old-fashioned, but there is something
almost redemptive about looking through—rather
than into—a smartphone "screen" to see the
real, analogue world anew, as Lothar Böttcher's
Pocket Lens encourages us to do.   *— AC*

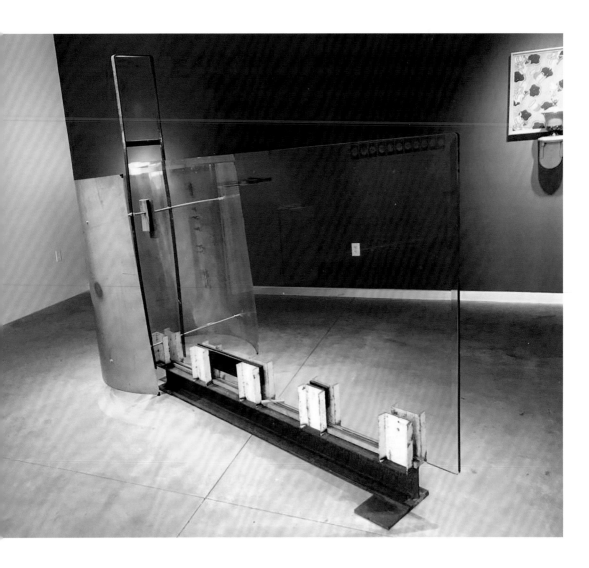

SHAUN CONROY

United States (b. 1972)

ClydeStew1

Plate glass, steel, wood, mallets

152 x 152 x 250 cm

SJJ, BL

Glass has an ability to convey sound in a particularly soft way. Music and glass are combined in Conroy's *ClydeStew1*. Here, Conroy explores his personal relationship with glass, drawing upon his musical background.   — *SJJ*

ALICIA EGGERT

United States (b. 1981)

All the Light You See

Neon, custom controller, steel

304 x 244 x 183 cm

Photo: Ryan Strand Greenberg

BL

With a debt to Bruce Nauman, whose neon signs catapulted the material to the forefront of contemporary art in the 1960s, *All the Light You See* is a poignant, didactic work that fluctuates between illuminating the words "All the Light You See Is from the Past" and "All You See Is Past." It is scientifically accurate and emotive simultaneously.   *— BL*

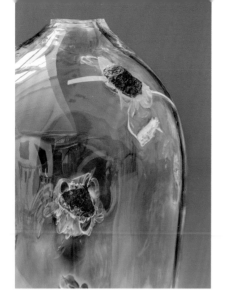 

MARIA BANG ESPERSEN

Denmark (b. 1981)

Things Change

Blown glass; brick, rock, window glass

53 x 300 x 95 cm

Photo: Dorte Krogh

AC, SJJ, BL, SJS

"Infected" with foreign materials—rocks, pieces of brick, and window glass—Maria Bang Espersen's blown glass vessels slowly crack and disintegrate over time, offering an achingly beautiful reading on mortality and impermanence.   *— AC*

NICKOLAUS FRUIN

United States (b. 1986)

High RI Bottles

Glass canes created from highly refractive, artist-formulated glass and commercially available soda-lime blowing glass, blown

28 x 60 x 11 cm

Photo: Mercedes Jelinek

AC, SJJ, SJS

Look at these bottles quickly and you might think there is nothing much to see. Slow down, and you'll notice a subtle and complex pattern of twisted clear-on-clear cane just visible throughout. To make these vessels, Fruin used traditional Venetian blowing techniques to combine two colorless glasses: a standard soda-lime and a *duro* glass he formulated himself. The pattern appears because these glasses have different indexes of refraction. A remarkable study of subtlety and chemical possibility. —*SJS*

MARTINO GAMPER

Italy (b. 1971)

for J. & L. LOBMEYR Austria

"Neo" Tumblers

Blown lead-free crystal, cut, engraved, painted,
lustered, gilded, sandblasted

9.7 x 9 x 9 cm

Photo: Lobmeyr/Klaus Fritsch

AC, BL, SJS

Like his well-known "100 Chairs in 100 Days"
project, for which he mixed and matched parts
of discarded furniture to create new seating
pieces, Martino Gamper cut, engraved, polished,
sandblasted, painted, and gilded archetypal
double old-fashioned whiskey tumblers to
produce this virtuosic new series.   — *AC*

KATHERINE GRAY
United States (b. 1965)

Iridescent Aura Diptych II

Blown and slumped glass; aluminum frame

51 x 51 x 2.5 cm

Photo: Andrew K. Thompson

SJJ, BL, SJS

In *Iridescent Aura Diptych II*, the properties of iridescent glass activate the viewer and the work simultaneously. The work appears to shift and radiate as the viewer approaches and engages it, much in keeping with Op Art concerns. In so doing, Gray captures the ephemeral phenomena of the rainbow, distilling it into a simplified, thoughtful experience.   — *BL*

JIRO KAMATA

Japan (b. 1978)

Ghost

Mirror, quartz coating, silver

60 x 40 x 1 cm

SJJ, BL, SJS

Ghost slyly insinuates its adornment on the viewer. A mirrored brooch displayed on a mirror, it fragments the viewer, disrupting the common act of self-inspection with an unexpected additional ornament. It is a psychological work that commands engagement, reflection, and adornment.   — BL

KARINA MALLING
Denmark (b. 1982)

Transcendence

Glass and vitreous materials from artist-made batch formulations, cast/melted, cut, chiseled, polished

120 x 200 x 30 cm

AC, SJJ, BL, SJS

Still life has always been used to display objects with familiarity: dead animals, flowers, porcelain, or man-made objects within a common genre. Malling's still life is a display of aesthetic experimentation with phenomenology, with the materiality of glass, and with color and shape.   *— SJJ*

AMIE McNEEL

United States (b. 1964)

Portal, projection #2

Slumped glass

35.6 x 35.6 x 35.6 cm

SJJ, BL

Glass is one of the materials best suited to
distilling the wonder of natural phenomena. In
Portal, Projection #2, the material is absent, but
the mystery remains. It deftly courts attention
to beauty and awe of the unknown.   *— BL*

SEAN MERCHANT

United States (b. 1982)

Corporal Mercies 1–3 (offering hospitality to strangers, clothing the naked, visiting the sick)

Kiln-formed plate glass, mirrored

45.7 x 144.8 x 2.5 cm

AC, SJJ, BL, SJS

With reference to stained glass as a mode of expression, Merchant's piece uses phenomenology and the reflections and other effects that appear when glass is bent and manipulated. In this way, the visual presence of the piece is twofold. Its impact is as much on the wall as it is in the reflection on the floor.   — SJJ

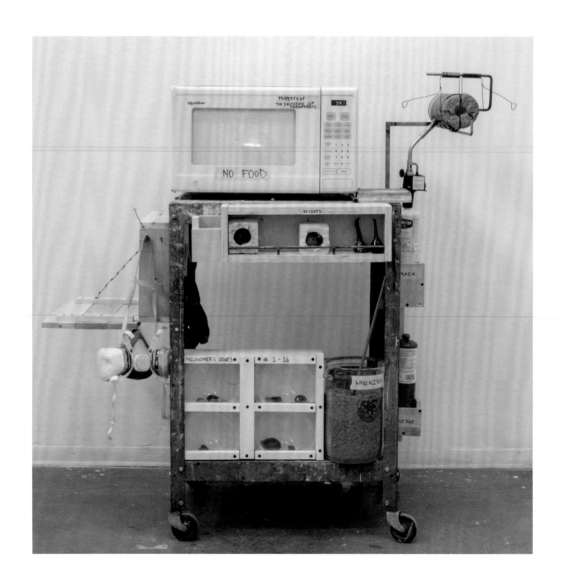

LUKAS MILANAK

United States (b. 1995)

Mobile Alchemy Research Station (M.A.R.S.)

Found objects

137.2 x 137 x 76 cm

Photo: Luke Hall Media

AC, BL, SJS

Venturing into the realm of design fiction, Lukas Milanak's *Mobile Alchemy Research Station (M.A.R.S.)* speculates on a post-cataclysmic future in which DIY hackers revive the medieval alchemist's quest for the elusive philosopher's stone. — *AC*

MICHAL MOTYCKA

Czech Republic (b. 1974)

Gravity

Metalized plate glass; mirror, metal construction

170 x 170 x 30 cm

AC, SJJ, BL, SJS

The construction of *Gravity* appears simple: two mirrors, mounted at an angle to each other, are disguised under a curved sheet of glass. But the experience of this piece is anything but. By reorganizing and layering reflections, *Gravity* seems to amplify the experience of everything around it, reinvesting the everyday with a sense of mystery.   — *SJS*

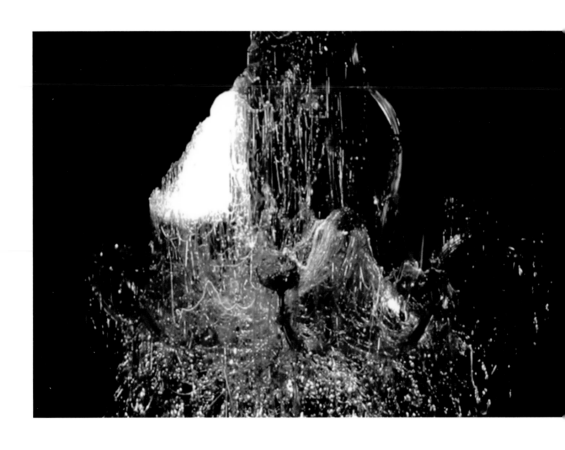

AARON PEXA

United States (b. 1976)

The Lucent Parlor Chapter 1

Video, 40 min.

SJJ, BL, SJS

In *The Lucent Parlor Chapter 1*, threads of brilliant molten glass re-enact the flicker of candlelight as they are unwound (and ultimately wound) around the body of a 19th-century chandelier. In replacing the chandelier's native candlelight with the glow of molten glass, Pexa evokes the feeling of the past while maintaining its unknowable otherness. It is an uncanny intervention that captures the mystery of the glassworking process.   —*SJS*

TOMÁŠ PROKOP

Czech Republic (b. 1992)

Parting (second version)

Sheet glass, asphalt

53 x 65 x 120 cm

BL, SJS

Elegant and powerful, *Parting (second version)* is a study in contrasts: the fluid and the rigid, the brittle and the supple, the street and the window, the terrestrial and the heavenly.   *—SJS*

ANNA RILEY

United States (b. 1992)

Transparency in Which Certain Things Are Crossed Out

Utility shelf, modified beer bottle glass, ceramic crucibles, furnace glass, industrial molds, blown glass

Overall: 289.6 x 124.5 x 139.7 cm

Photo: Gabriel Cosma

AC, SJJ, BL, SJS

Experimenting with matter and searching for originality in raw materials, Riley explores how recycled glass, sand, limestone, and oyster shells can be transformed into a new substance. Riley's project is a library of material knowledge, but also a way to speak out about her concerns regarding the environment and the world we live in.   *—SJJ*

JEROEN VERHOEVEN
The Netherlands (b. 1976)
and JOEP VERHOEVEN
The Netherlands (b. 1976)

"Bubble" Cabinet

Iridized borosilicate glass

102 x 92 x 72 cm

Courtesy of the artists and Blain | Southern

Photo: Prudence Cuming Associates, 2017

AC

The way it so tentatively captures fragility, and at such a scale and with such precision, gives the Verhoevens' "Bubble" Cabinet an air of impossibility that one has to appreciate.   *— AC*

BOHYUN YOON

United States and Republic of Korea
(b. 1976)

Family II

Cast glass; motorized pedestal; spotlight

266.7 x 335 x 427 cm

AC, BL, SJS

In *Family II*, a spinning mass of cast glass projects a human silhouette onto the wall. As it turns, the profile transforms from the artist's to his wife's to his child's and back again. Surrounded by subtly shifting refracting rainbows, the piece is an evocation of wonder at the materiality of glass, the immateriality of light, and the unknowable mystery of the family connection.   — SJS

Artists' Contact Information

TAMÁS ÁBEL pp. 90, 91
Budapest, Hungary
tamasabelglass@gmail.com
www.tamasabel.com

JAMES AKERS pp. 154, 155
Arlington, Texas, U.S.A.
jamesakersart@gmail.com

MIYA ANDO pp. 16, 17
Long Island City, New York, U.S.A.
studio@miyaando.com
www.miyaando.com

ATELIER NL pp. 18, 19
**LONNY VAN RYSWYCK
and NADINE STERK**
Eindhoven, The Netherlands
lonny@ateliernl.com
www.ateliernl.com

FLAVIE AUDI pp. 156, 157
London, England, U.K.
www.flavieaudi.com

KATE BAKER pp. 112, 113
Sydenham, New South Wales,
Australia
kate@katebaker.com.au
www.katebaker.com.au

ANS BAKKER pp. 20, 21
Amersfoort, The Netherlands
info@ansbakker.nl
www.ansbakker.nl

G. WILLIAM BELL pp. 50, 51
Nexø, Denmark
g.williambellglass@hotmail.com
www.diameter34.com

STINE BIDSTRUP pp. 52, 53
Copenhagen, Denmark
mail@stinebidstrup.dk
www.stinebidstrup.dk

JULI BOLAÑOS-DURMAN
pp. 158, 159
Edinburgh, Scotland, U.K.
julibd@gmail.com
www.julibd.com

**MONICA BONVICINI
for Berengo Studio** pp. 92, 93
Murano, Italy
www.berengo.com

TORD BOONTJE pp. 186, 187
London, England, U.K.
https://tordboontje.com

LOTHAR BÖTTCHER pp. 188, 189
Pretoria, Republic of South Africa
lothar@lotharbottcher.com
http://lotharbottcher.com

**ERWAN BOUROULLEC
and RONAN BOUROULLEC
for Iittala Inc.** pp. 54, 55
Iittala, Finland
www.iittala.com

DYLAN BRAMS pp. 114, 115
Portland, Oregon, U.S.A.
dylan.brams@gmail.com
www.dylanbrams.com

SARAH BRILAND pp. 22, 23
Richmond, Virginia, U.S.A.
www.sbriland.com

**STEFANO BULLO
and MATTEO SILVERIO** pp. 56, 57
Murano, Italy
info@vetrateartistichemurano.com
www.vetrateartistichemurano.com

NACHO CARBONELL pp. 24, 25
Eindhoven, The Netherlands
http://nachocarbonell.com

KEERYONG CHOI pp. 58, 59
Edinburgh, Scotland, U.K.

DAVID COLTON pp. 160, 161
Chesterfield Gallery
New York, New York, U.S.A.
simon@thechesterfieldgallery.com
http://thechesterfieldgallery.com

SHAUN CONROY pp. 190, 191
North Kingstown, Rhode Island,
U.S.A.
conroyglass@yahoo.com
http://conroyglass.com

MATTHEW CURTIS pp. 60, 61
Queanbeyan, New South Wales,
Australia
mail@curtisglassart.com
www.curtisglassart.com

DEBORAH CZERESKO pp. 94, 95
New York, New York, U.S.A.
deborahczeresko@gmail.com
http://deborahczeresko.com

ANDREA DA PONTE pp. 26, 27
Buenos Aires, Argentina
andreadapontevidrio@gmail.com
www.andreadapontevidrio.com

DORIS DARLING pp. 96, 97
Vienna, Austria
hello@dorisdarling.at
www.dorisdarling.at

MATTHEW DAY PEREZ pp. 62, 63
Brooklyn, New York, U.S.A.
matthew.d.perez@gmail.com
www.matthewdayperez.com

**ROSS DELANO, ERIKH VARGO,
and BRAD PATOCKA** pp. 98, 99
Corning, New York, U.S.A.

**DAVID DERKSEN
for Tre Product** pp. 64, 65
Czerwonak, Poland
contact@treproduct.com
www.treproduct.com

JITKA KOLBE-RŮŽIČKOVÁ
pp. 128, 129
Prague, Czech Republic
jitkaruzickova@volny.cz
www.jitkakolbe.cz

PEADAR LAMB pp. 170, 171
Cork, Republic of Ireland
info@peadarlamb.com
www.peadarlamb.com

CAROLINE LANDAU pp. 36, 37
Wernersville, Pennsylvania, U.S.A.
carolinelandau25@gmail.com
www.carolinelandau.com

DANNY LANE pp. 130, 131
London, England, U.K.
info@dannylane.co.uk
www.dannylane.co.uk

HELEN LEE pp. 74, 75
Madison, Wisconsin, U.S.A.
helenylee@gmail.com
www.pink-noise.org

SHAYNA LEIB pp. 132, 133
Madison, Wisconsin, U.S.A.
www.shaynaleib.com

JAMES MAGAGULA pp. 38, 39
Ngwenya, Kingdom of eSwatini
(formerly Swaziland)
ngwenya@ngwenyaglass.co.sz
https://ngwenyaglass.co.sz

KARINA MALLING pp. 204, 205
Aarhus, Denmark
www.karinamalling.com

GEOFFREY MANN pp. 134, 135
Edinburgh, Scotland, U.K.
info@geoffreymann.com
http://geoffreymann.com

AMIE McNEEL pp. 206, 207
Seattle, Washington, U.S.A.
amiemcneel@mac.com
http://amiemcneel.com

SEAN MERCHANT pp. 208, 209
Brunswick, Ohio, U.S.A.
sean.r.merchant@gmail.com
www.seanrmerchant.com

LUKAS MILANAK pp. 210, 211
Willow Street, Pennsylvania,
U.S.A.
luke.milanak@gmail.com
http://2014117.wixsite.com
/lukasartglass/artist-info

MICHAL MOTYCKA pp. 212, 213
Prague, Czech Republic
m.motycka@habena.cz

**STANISLAV MULLER
and RADKA MULLEROVA**
pp. 172, 173
Teplice, Czech Republic
info@stanislavmuller.com
www.stanislavmuller.com

FREDRIK NIELSEN pp. 102, 103
Stockholm, Sweden
fredrik@fredriknielsen.se
www.fredriknielsen.se

AYA OKI pp. 76, 77
Victorville, California, U.S.A.
ayapon_1214@hotmail.com
http://cargocollective.com/ayaoki

SHARYN O'MARA pp. 174, 175
Philadelphia, Pennsylvania, U.S.A.
www.sharynomara.com

MOMOO OMURO pp. 78, 79
Tokyo, Tokyo, Japan
momoomro@gmail.com
http://momoo.jp

**ZORA PALOVÁ
and ŠTĚPÁN PALA** pp. 136, 137
Bratislava, Slovakia
zora.palova@pala.sk

SUZANNE PECK pp. 104, 105
Essex Fells, New Jersey, U.S.A.
suzannepeck@gmail.com
www.exhalewithvigor.org

AARON PEXA pp. 214, 215
Providence, Rhode Island, U.S.A.
www.aaronpexa.com

TOMÁŠ PROKOP pp. 216, 217
Žd'ár nad Sázavou, Czech
Republic
prokop-tomas@seznam.cz
www.works.io/tomas-prokop

LAURA PUSKA pp. 138, 139
Helsinki, Finland
www.puska.me

KIRSTIE REA pp. 40, 41
Queanbeyan, New South Wales,
Australia
kirstierea@yahoo.com.au

NATE RICCIUTO pp. 176, 177
Columbus, Ohio, U.S.A.
nate.ricciuto@gmail.com
www.natericciuto.com

ANNA RILEY pp. 218, 219
Hoover, Alabama, U.S.A.
www.annariley.org

TOMO SAKAI pp. 178, 179
Worcester, Massachusetts,
U.S.A.
tomo@cruzesakai.com
www.cruzesakai.com

RUI SASAKI Cover, p. 245
Kanazawa, Ishikawa, Japan
https://rui-sasaki.com

MEGAN STELLJES pp. 106, 107
Lakewood, Washington, U.S.A.
megan.stelljes@gmail.com
www.meganstelljes.com

AUSTIN STERN pp. 140, 141
Seattle, Washington, U.S.A.
sternglass@gmail.com
www.austinstern.com

C. MATTHEW SZÖSZ pp. 142, 143
Seattle, Washington, U.S.A.
matthewszosz@gmail.com
www.matthewszosz.com

CHRISTINE TARKOWSKI
pp. 80, 81
Chicago, Illinois, U.S.A.
www.christinetarkowski.com

ANGELA THWAITES pp. 180, 181
Croydon, England, U.K.
www.angelathwaites.com

BLANCHE TILDEN pp. 144, 145
Carlton, Victoria, Australia
blanche_tilden@outlook.com
www.blanchetilden.com.au

CECILIA UNTARIO pp. 146, 147
Jakarta, Indonesia
patricia.oen@gmail.com

SYLVIE VANDENHOUCKE
pp. 82, 83
Tienen, Belgium
info@sylvievandenhoucke.com

**JEROEN VERHOEVEN
and JOEP VERHOEVEN**
pp. 220, 221
London, England, U.K.
info@blainsouthern.com
www.blainsouthern.com

NORWOOD VIVIANO pp. 84, 85
Plainwell, Michigan, U.S.A.
www.norwoodviviano.com

QIN WANG pp. 86, 87
Shanghai, China
wangqinstudio@126.com

CHIEMI WATANABE pp. 42, 43
Waki, Yamaguchi, Japan
chiemi3175@yahoo.co.jp

IDA WIETH pp. 44, 45
Ebeltoft, Denmark
idawieth@gmail.com
www.idawieth.com

**ERWIN WURM
for Berengo Studio** pp. 182, 183
Murano, Italy
www.berengo.com

DUSTIN YELLIN pp. 148, 149
Brooklyn, New York, U.S.A.
info@dustinyellin.com
www.dustinyellin.com

BOHYUN YOON pp. 222, 223
Richmond, Virginia, U.S.A.
bobobo22@gmail.com
www.bohyunyoon.com

HE ZHAO pp. 150, 151
Hangzhou, China
1011778129@qq.com

MARK ZIRPEL pp. 108, 109
Seattle, Washington, U.S.A.
mzirpel@uw.edu
http://markzirpel.com

TOOTS ZYNSKY pp. 46, 47
Providence, Rhode Island, U.S.A.
www.tootszynsky.com

Curators' Perspectives

Beth Lipman

Susanne Jøker Johnsen

Aric Chen

Susie J. Silbert

ARIC CHEN (AC)
Curator-at-Large
M+, Hong Kong SAR, China

Participating in an exhibition of glass has been, in many ways, a welcome hiatus for me.

For six years, my focus as a curator at M+, a new museum for visual culture in Hong Kong, was on constructing and revisiting design histories through less-trodden socio-historical perspectives, and in other projects, I've tended to explore more generally an array of contemporary questions. Nowadays, many curators rely on such frameworks—on seeing design, and design objects, through topical narratives—but a consequence of this is that we all too often lose sight of the lens that's been there all along: the medium, or material.

As an appreciator of glass, rather than an expert, I have found New Glass Review to be a reminder of the richness still to be found in material-based perspectives. The projects submitted were worthy successors to longstanding explorations of glass as a technique, process, and craft; as both a medium and a subject; as an artistic endeavor and a conceptual foil; and as an artifact of current social trends: with the spreading legalization of marijuana, bongs seemed to come up a lot in our discussions.

And yet, while the expansiveness of glass on its own terms—as an autonomous site of inquiry—remains readily apparent, the possibilities of glass as an application offer further room for investigation. In architecture, one thinks of the sublime optical-glass stage of Hiroshi Sugimoto's recently completed Enoura Observatory in Japan, or of MVRDV's Chanel flagship store in Amsterdam, with its glass bricks and architectural detailing transforming its historical facade into a captivating phantom of itself. Made possible by technical innovations, both projects show how the architectural use of glass continues to push the technological development of glass, while the reverse also holds true: consider Neri Oxman's research into 3-D-printed glass and her efforts to apply it on an architectural scale.

Like Oxman, others are creating work that lies at the intersection of research, technology, and speculation. Marjan van Aubel's *Cyanometer* lights for Swarovski combine solar cells with specially cut crystals that improve their efficiency. Frank Kolkman's *Dreammachine*, also for

Swarovski, is an exercise in neural-environmental synthesis that synchronizes one's brain waves with sound and light patterns emitted by the crystal rods of an immersive chamber.

Indeed, even when driven by the most technical concerns, at the cutting edge of technology, the discursive future of glass remains bright. Here I think of Motosuke Mandai's *Soundscape* for Asahi, an installation of suspended glass panes that emitted audio recordings through the vibrations of the glass itself—once again situating glass between the material and immaterial, the physical and experiential, and as both a starting point and a medium.

More information: www.mplus.org.hk

Dreammachine (Swarovski Designers of the Future 2018)
Austria, Swarovski, 2018

FRANK KOLKMAN (Dutch, b. 1989)

72 Swarovski crystal prisms, anodized aluminum mechanics, Plexiglas case; daybed: foam, upholstered with Kvadrat Lift

110 x 90 x 74 cm; daybed: 34 x 90 x 166 cm

Swarovski Corporate Archive

Photo: Swarovski

Glass II
Italy, Milan, installation for the Milan Triennale, 2017

THE MEDIATED MATTER GROUP (MIT Media Lab)
Neri Oxman (American-Israeli, b. 1976), project and group director, in collaboration with Lexus Milan Design Week

3-D-printed, optically transparent glass; internal lighting system, dark mirrors

Columns (each): 300 cm

Photo: © MIT Media Lab

Crystal Houses (Chanel Flagship Store)
The Netherlands, Amsterdam, and Italy, Resana, Poesia (casting), 2016

MVRDV (principal in charge, **Winy Maas** [Dutch, b. 1959]), co-architects: Gietermans & Van Dijk Wim Gietermans, Arjan Bakker, Tuğrul Avuçlu

Cast glass bricks, glass window frames

840 square meters (620m^2 Retail and 220m^2 Residential)

Photo: © MVRDV 2018

Optical Glass Stage, Enoura Observatory
Japan, Odawara, 2017

HIROSHI SUGIMOTO (Japanese, b. 1948)

Optical glass, *kakeukuri* frame of Hinoki cypress

Stage: 540 x 750 cm

Odawara Art Foundation, Kanagawa, Japan

Photo: © Odawara Art Foundation

Cyanometer (Swarovski Designers
of the Future 2017)
Austria, Swarovski, 2017

MARJAN VAN AUBEL (Dutch, b. 1985)

Chandelier: 160 Swarovski Opal crystals, stainless steel
frame, suspension rope; Solar Powerbank: Swarovski
crystal, 3-D-printed frame

Chandelier: 6 x 120 cm, Solar Powerbank: 30 x 8 cm

Swarovski Corporate Archive

Photo: Swarovski

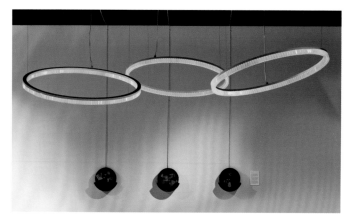

SUSANNE JØKER JOHNSEN (SJJ)
Head of Exhibitions
The Royal Danish Academy of Fine Arts
Schools of Architecture, Design,
    and Conservation
Copenhagen, Denmark

As a maker and curator of European glass, I am deeply connected to glass as a material and as an idea.

Therefore, it was a true pleasure to review the overwhelming number of applications submitted to "New Glass Now." Although each artist and craftsperson came from a distinct cultural background and tradition, all of the works centered around the common material of glass. Some started from raw materials and processed them in experimental ways, in what seems to me a search to get closer to the material and its origin. Others were more concerned with form and took more sculptural or architectural approaches. There were conceptual installations and humorous video works, but also politically charged art works that, despite being aesthetically appealing, focus on themes such as gender, the environment, and sustainability. I am excited about the variety in these approaches, especially when material, skill, and idea come together in a meaningful way.

Wise hands describes the craftsman who has years of experience working with a given material and is intimately familiar with personal style and technique, combined with in-depth knowledge of the unique properties of the material. Glassmaking is mesmerizing to watch, and the process can be thrilling to the maker. But how can this be captured in a way that makes sense, not only to the maker, but also to the viewer? I believe that skill, idea, and sophisticated use of material can make the poetry of the material arise, if the artist has wise hands.

Bjørn Friborg (Denmark) and Terese William Waenerlund (Sweden) are artists and craftsmen who use the unique properties of glass to tell a personal story in an aesthetically interesting way. In *Implosion*, Friborg utilizes the material's full potential. The title emphasizes the energy in both the inner and outer shape of the piece. Waenerlund has invented a new way of glassmaking that she calls *burn out*. She mixes glass powder with such other materials as fabric, chemicals, and metal, and then burns out the natural materials with a torch. What is left is the fired glass powder in a new, rough, and fragile state, almost like foaming ceramic glazing held together by the metal grit and frame. The results are both stunning and aesthetically strong.

While one-of-a-kind objects in glass are not new, artists are using their craftsmanship as a societal mirror in a new way to express their opinions. Their craftsmanship is a conceptual framework from which their works emanate, with the titles serving as directives or captions for the pieces. *The Eternal Emigrant* by Ilya and Emilia Kabakov (Russia) is one example. The piece depicts a man stuck in his climb over a wall, revealing a personal and political statement about immigration. The fragility and strength of the glass underline the Kabakovs' sentiment and approach toward a topic that is central to our century and perhaps all the centuries before. The work was made a few years ago, before the mass migrations of our present moment. It reflects the artists' lived experience in the psychologically demanding process of moving physically or mentally, not belonging anywhere, being in no man's land.

The art works and projects in this edition of *New Glass Review* offer messages and comments that are often personal and arise from the artists' individual interests, experiences, or journeys. The works and their messages pose questions that are relevant to us all—conceptually, aesthetically, and artistically.

More information: susannejohnsen.com

Department of Voids; Evidence of Enculturation
China, Czech Republic, Denmark, and Germany, 2015–2018
BENANDSEBASTIAN
Ben Clement (British, b. 1981)
and Sebastian de la Cour (Danish, b. 1980)

Transport case: wood, leather, brass, velvet, paper, wax; glass insert

Case: 23 x 23 x 52 cm; insert: 18 x 18 x 48 cm

Shanghai Museum of Glass; 21st Century Museum of Contemporary Art, Kanazawa, Ishikawa, Japan

Photo: Courtesy of the artists

Speed Crafting Jam
Sweden, Stockholm, Konstfack, 2015
MARKUS EMILSSON (Swedish, b. 1973)
Performance or participant-based
performance
90 min.
Photo: Courtesy of the artist

Implosion
2018
BJØRN FRIBORG (Danish, b. 1983)
Sculptured glass
50 x 50 x 50 cm
Private collection
Photo: Mattias Tiedermann

The Eternal Emigrant
Italy, Venice, Berengo Studio for Glasstress, 2013
EMILIA KABAKOV (Russian-American, b. 1945)
and ILYA KABAKOV (Russian-American, b. 1933)
Cast glass
51 x 35 x 2 cm
Private collection
Photo: Berengo Studio

Famiglia
Sweden, Kungsbacka, 2016
TERESE WILLIAM WAENERLUND
(Swedish, b. 1982)
Glass, metal, textile, epoxy
145 x 195 cm
Private collection
Photo: Andreas Påhlsson

BETH LIPMAN (BL)
Artist
Sheboygan Falls, Wisconsin

When I was in residence at the Smithsonian National Museum of Natural History, investigating paleoflora and climate change, I chanced upon a devil's corkscrew, a wondrous fossil made by an ancient form of beaver called a *Palaeocastor*.

Its shape called to mind a Solomonic column, but its size defied the proportions of any known architecture. This object was unknown and exotic to me, an unfamiliar abyss. Long after the initial encounter, it remains vividly imprinted on my mind, demanding attention even now that I am familiar with the form.

Reviewing the submissions to "New Glass Now" felt similar to discovering the *Palaeocastor*'s work, but with the added pressure of wanting the selections to spark a comparable sense of discovery in the public. Against the backdrop of mining for "newness," and the variety of forms that can take, I was concerned with making selections that represented the wide-ranging diversity found in the field right now, at this critical time in history. These concerns created a much-needed road map for decision-making and resulted in choices that continue to

confound. There were strongly resolved objects by highly accomplished artists that nonetheless were left on the cutting-room floor, replaced by those of artists previously unknown to me. The necessarily whirlwind-like process of curating a coherent selection from so many entries provoked its own mysterious alchemy.

I was also reminded of the incredible power of glass to encode many disparate meanings in simple objects. Take, for example, the cover of Yoko Ono's 1981 album *Season of Glass*, which employs two simple glass objects—spectacles and a water glass—to make a profound statement about senseless violence and loss. Splashed with blood, the spectacles had belonged to John Lennon, her partner, who had been murdered the year before. The featureless drinking glass, shown half empty, represents the life-giving qualities of water and Ono's perseverance following her personal—and our cultural—tragedy.

Less dramatic, but no less powerful, is the Iraqi-Kurdish artist Hiwa K's use of reflectivity to amplify his experience as a refugee and migrant. His *Pre-Image (Blind as the Mother Tongue)* documents his use of an improvised navigational tool, consisting of a cane-like stick mounted with mirrors, that he uses by balancing it on his head while walking. The mirrors fragment his view—and therefore his understanding of the city—while nonetheless assisting in his wayfinding.

In each of these works, glass is used simply and provocatively, providing the connective tissue between the personal and the global. Like so many of the pieces included in this exhibition, they relate to broader cultural concerns, providing a topical relevance that is imperative to the health of the field. Overall, the New Glass experience demonstrates the continued relevance of objects to our lives and their capacity to act as catalysts motivating and inspiring new modes of thinking and expression.

More information: www.bethlipman.com

Monir Farmanfarmaian in Her Studio
Iran, Tehran, 1975
MONIR FARMANFARMAIAN (Iranian, b. 1924)
Photo: Courtesy of the artist

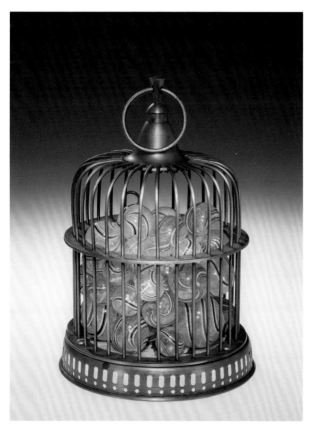

Pre-Image
(Blind as the Mother Tongue)
2017

HIWA K (Iraqi, b. 1975)

Single-channel high-definition video, 16:9, color, sound (in English), 17 min., 40 sec.

Berlin, Germany

Photo: Courtesy of the artist and KOW, Berlin, Germany

Richard Posner Marbles
in Birdcage Reliquary
United States, Whidbey Island, Washington, 2011

RICHARD MARQUIS
(American, b. 1945)
Assisted by Brian Pike (American, b. 1958)

Glass marbles containing cremated remains; metal birdcage

23 x 16.2 cm

The Corning Museum of Glass, Corning, New York (2012.4.83, gift of Ralph and Eugenia Potkin, Petra Korink, and Richard Marquis)

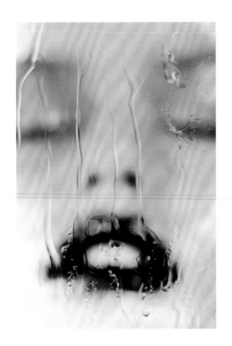

Black Orchid
2012
MARILYN MINTER
(American, b. 1948)
C-print
218.4 x 144.8 cm
Photo: Courtesy of the artist
and Salon 94, New York

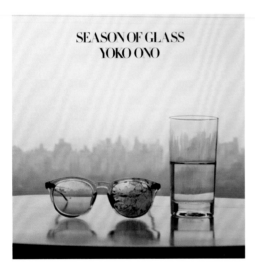

Season of Glass Album Cover
1981
YOKO ONO (Japanese, b. 1933)
31.4 x 31.4 cm
Photo and concept: Yoko Ono

Springtime Anytime
United States, Sheboygan, Wisconsin,
Kohler Arts Center, 2017
JOEL OTTERSON (American, b. 1959)
Plated brass, enameled glass, found object
67.3 x 44.5 x 10.2 cm
Collection of the artist
Photo: Courtesy of the artist

SUSIE J. SILBERT (SJS)
Curator of Modern and Contemporary Glass
The Corning Museum of Glass

As a true believer in glass and the avenues of inquiry it opens for artists, designers, and thinkers of all kinds, I find nothing is more fulfilling than New Glass Review and the annual peek it provides into creative practices around the globe.

But my privileged view also reminds me of what is missing. Even as these pages and the accompanying exhibition show the diversity of contemporary glass more than ever before, to a broader audience than ever before, I can't help but think about the types of work that are not contained within these pages. Whether because they can't be hemmed in by paper or the constraints of physical space, or because they otherwise fall outside the vast sweep of the New Glass Review process, there are yawning gaps where other work should be.

Pipemaking—one of the most important and active areas of contemporary glass—is almost entirely neglected in these pages. This is not because of disinterest on the part of the panel, but rather because pipemakers seem to have edited themselves out of the process. Of the more than 1,400 entries, only five came from pipemakers, and even then, the pieces they submitted were,

more often than not, sculptural representations of their functional ware. To me, it is a sign of a continuing feeling of second-class citizenship brought on by a mainstream glass world that for too long looked down its nose at this incredible, culturally relevant art form.

Mike Raman's *PipeGeist* is a strong example of the way contemporary pipemaking has grown up while the rest of the glass world averted its eyes. In the style of an early Josiah McElheny, Raman has reproduced many of the most iconic pipes in the field. In place of the obliterating purity of McElheny's modern white, however, Raman's reproductions are a deep black, residue of the field's continued black-sheep status.

Operating just outside the center of our object-focused view are organizations that use glass as a vehicle for forging connections across cultural and class divides. One that particularly stands out is Berlin Glas and its Multaka Workshops, a partnership with Multaka: Museum as Meeting Point. This larger organization trains "New Berliners" (the preferred term for refugees to this German city) as museum guides, using individual objects to spark dialogue and facilitate the exchange of ideas between groups that might not otherwise meet. The Multaka Workshops at Berlin Glas work in a similar way, using the material as the meeting point for locals and New Berliners alike. "The underlying significance," explains Nadania Idriss, founder of Berlin Glas, "is that working in collaboration—working together—doesn't just broaden someone's capacity to learn a new skill but has the ability to foster a culture of peace."[1]

Similarly, New Glass Review is a meeting point—a catalyst—accelerating the pace of change and exchange in a field that is always shifting, moving, and working toward unknown horizons of exploration and discovery. I have framed the examples above as gaps in an otherwise comprehensive look at contemporary glass, but really I see them as openings. This exhibition, this catalog, are mere moments in a series of unfurling narratives about the possibilities of material, hand, and mind. I look forward to the future.

1. E-mail message to the author, January 5, 2019.

Susie J. Silbert joined the Corning Museum in 2016. More information:www.cmog.org/bio/susie-silbert

Berlin Glas–Multaka Workshops, Tour of the Museum of Islamic Art, Pergamon Museum
Germany, Berlin, December 2018
ANDREA BECKER (German)
Photo: Berlin Glas e.V.

Opposite:

Untitled (White)
United States, Seattle, Washington, 2000
JOSIAH McELHENY (American, b. 1966)
Blown glass vessels; wooden case with light box
56.5 x 218.6 x 40.7 cm
The Corning Museum of Glass, Corning, New York
(2000.4.9, the 15th Rakow Commission)

PipeGeist
United States, Burlington, Vermont,
Bern Gallery, 2018
MICHAEL RAMAN (American, b. 1994)
Blown glass; display cabinet, lighting
39.4 x 125.7 x 35.6 cm
Private collection
Photo: Connor McHugh

Five New Berliners Explore Moldmaking during Berlin Glas–Multaka Workshop
Germany, Berlin, June 2017
Photo: Berlin Glas e.V.

The 2018 Rakow Commission: Rui Sasaki

Rui Sasaki is an artist and educator from Japan who uses an array of materials, including resin, ice, light, performance, and especially glass, to highlight subtle aspects of everyday life. As an itinerant artist, pursuing opportunities around the globe, she has often created work that deals with the slipperiness of the concept of "home" and with the idea of creating spaces of belonging. Her more recent works address the weather, drawing viewers' attention to the subtle qualities of sunshine and rain and the emotional states they provoke.

Sasaki's Rakow Commission, *Liquid Sunshine/ I am a Pluviophile*, distills her interest in weather. A room-size installation, the piece consists of more than 200 blown glass "raindrops," each embedded with small dots of phosphorescent material that absorb simulated sunlight. Installed in a darkened room with broad-spectrum lights regulated by a motion detector, the raindrops are charged only when the room is empty. As soon as a viewer approaches the piece, the lights turn off, leaving only the glowing outlines of the raindrops visible. Over time, the glowing phosphorescent glass dims, the way the memory of sunshine fades during the dark days of winter.   — *SJS*

Liquid Sunshine/I am a Pluviophile
Japan, Kanazawa, Ishikawa, 2018
RUI SASAKI Japan (b. 1984)
Blown glass with phosphorescent material, broad-spectrum UV lights, motion detector
335.3 x 426.7 x 365.8 cm
The Corning Museum of Glass, Corning, New York (2018.6.2, the 33rd Rakow Commission, purchased with funds from the Juliette K. and Leonard S. Rakow Endowment Fund)
Photo: Yasushi Ichikawa

The following interview was conducted via Skype and was recorded at the artist's home in Kanazawa, Japan, on June 16, 2018. It has been edited and condensed.

SJS: *How did you decide to become an artist?*

RS: I wanted to be a surgeon or an archaeologist when I was a kid, but I gave up. Then I was interested in water all the time. I always wanted to be under the water. Then I was wondering about how I can create something out of water all the time because I always want to touch water. But I can't, so I decided to try to find similar material to water. Then I found glass.

SJS: *You came to graduate school at the Rhode Island School of Design (RISD) in the United States. Why? How did it influence your thinking?*

RS: My graduation work, my B.F.A., I was really interested in design first. But decided to make more fine art so that I can put my concept in. . . . I was looking at a lot of universities in the United States and Europe and Scandinavia. In all the work I saw, I was really interested in the United States, so I decided to apply for university there. I did a postbac program, and then I did a two-year graduate program at RISD.

In the first year, my postbac, I was really confused because I studied design, and the RISD glass department, as you know, is very, very conceptual. I didn't know anything about fine art because I learned how to design. It's totally different; it was really hard. RISD taught me how I can dig deeper into my core interest. Even today, how I explore my work is based on how I learned, how it was taught to me, at RISD.

Rui Sasaki, recipient of the 33rd Rakow Commission.

SJS: *How do you go about developing your concepts into your pieces?*

RS: I'm very slow to work, but I really want to be comfortable and confident to find my interest. If my interest is not deep enough, I can't keep working. I really have to find my core and honest interest. I cannot lie to my work.

But for me it's also about touching glass, which is like blowing glass almost every day or twice a week. It's very important, even when I don't have any projects coming up. Seeing glass and touching glass all the time is very important for me because, oh, maybe I failed all those things, then I can find very interesting points through my failure, even if I don't know what to do with it. So I'm correcting all my failures and also I'm thinking, "Oh, I'm really interested in this concept." For example, I'm really interested in weather right now.

SJS: *You've had such an international practice from the beginning, getting on your feet, through now. Do you find that there are differences in approaches in the different countries? Do you feel like those different approaches find their way into your work?*

RS: After I came back to Japan, which was 2004 in the winter, after that it was so important for me to go outside of Japan. Because Japan is my country. I don't have any problem with the language. We don't have any issue of race. I don't have that much struggle. I'm trying to find my struggle and conflict all the time because that is the kind of stimulation I need to make my work.

Also, for my work, I'm exploring my intimacy and the subtle difference between the relationship of my body and the surroundings. So if I just live in Japan, I can't find it, the subtle difference. But if I go outside of Japan, I can find the difference—even a little, subtle difference—I can notice when I'm outside of Japan.

For example, I notice weather. It's crazy here, but when I went to Norway or Seattle or maybe even Corning, we're in a different country, but I can see the similar weather. At the same time, I can find similar points, but also I can see the subtle difference between.

SJS: *Did being in Norway influence the making of the piece your Rakow Commission is based on, and how do you think that translates into the work that you're doing for Corning or have done since then?*

RS: I did an artist residency program at S12 [Studio and Gallery] in Bergen, Norway, in April and May 2016, where it's the most rainy city in Europe. I chose that residency program because I was researching about weather.

In Japan, where I live right now, I was proposing using phosphorescent glass, which absorbs UV light like sunshine. I didn't know what kind of work I was going to make out of phosphorescent glass, but I knew that the weather in Bergen would inspire me, too. And that I could find [similarities to] Toyama, where I lived at that time, and also Bergen as well because it is a lot of rain, but maybe the humidity is different, how people enjoy rain, how people hate rain is maybe going to be different, and how people appreciate the sunshine may be different, so I was researching about it.

I couldn't find any books talking about rain or people interested in it. I was interviewing people: "How do you think about weather? How do you think about rain? How do you think about sunshine?" I feel that the weather really affects [people] emotionally and physically as well.

I found very interesting things in Bergen, then I decided to make work about how we can appreciate sunshine, how people can enjoy rain, or how I can change the perspective of enjoyment of rain because people think about rain in a negative way. Actually, I really enjoy rain so much because I can be calm, and also I like the rain sound. I really appreciate rain so much because I can appreciate even a little bit of sunshine after the rain's gone.

SJS: *Do you feel like you can do only certain things in certain weather?*

RS: I'm very affected by weather. If it is sunny days, I want to be more active, so I want to go outside. But on the rainy days . . . rainstorms make me so calm and relaxed. I can think well, somehow. And it seems like I thought about water. When I see raindrops on the window, that makes me very calm, and also raindrops magnify sound, and sometimes I can see a different perspective from raindrops. My five senses are more sensitive and can find a subtle difference in the rainy days. That's what I like about rain.

SJS: *Can you talk about, for you personally, how that affects your art work and the desire to find light.*

RS: Since we don't get much sunshine, even in summer, I'm more appreciative of subtle sunshine. After rainy days, if we get a little, little sunshine, it makes rainbows, so I can find the subtleness a lot after rainy days and cloudy days. That's why I have a desire to keep and record sunshine, even subtle [amounts], because we don't get much sunshine here. I want to show people that even if it's a little sunshine, we have sunshine. If I can keep or capture it, somehow I can show people that's how much we get the sunshine, even if you don't notice. That's why I started using phosphorescent material, because phosphorescents are very good at reacting to the weather.

This is a little off conversation, maybe, but I put my work everywhere in my room, so when I go back to home, I go, "This room has a very bright phosphorescent object. This room has not. So, I can tell how much sunshine goes through, coming through all my house, so I can see the difference. I live in a small house, but each room has a different reaction to the weather every day, so I kind of enjoy that.

SJS: *Rui, can you describe the piece that you're making for the Rakow Commission?*

RS: I'm making a room-size installation, and I'm making a lot of raindrop-shaped phosphorescent glass. The blown glass will be hanging from the ceiling, and some of the pieces are going to be on the floor. Visitors can go through a hallway to the room, and in the hallway, there is a motion detector. I use a broad-spectrum light, which is like a substitute sunshine light, to hang, and then, when people are in the special exhibition space, the light [turns] off. When people leave, it [turns back] on. When the light is off—when the viewers are in the space—the glass raindrop shapes glow and fade the longer viewers are in the space.

SJS: *The piece is about giving a gift of light or reinstilling the wonder—this sounds really cheesy as I'm saying it—but the wonder of being in light, especially after rain or something like that. . . .*

RS: I want the viewer to be, actually, weather. Because the motion detector is going to react to the visitor, if visitors are not coming, the broad-spectrum light—the false sun—is always on. That means a sunny day. If visitors are coming often, that means the sun light is not going to be on that much; that means cloudy days. So I try to make phosphorescent glass capture all the UV light from the solarium light. It's also why I'm interested to not just make an installation, but [also] to make it more interactive. This work reacts to and is influenced by how long viewers have been in the space and by the frequency of their visits. The brightness of the work depends on the viewers.

When people look at my work, they meditate because the phosphorescence kind of fades away, and people are more calm in the dark. Sometimes I feel like phosphorescent glass is a bit cheesy to use, because it glows in the dark, like a party, but I don't want people to think about that. I want them to spend time, to stay in here, because actually the fading out is very important for visitors to see. It's like how, on the rainy days, even a little sunshine comes through.

SJS: *Rui, you have been very lucky to receive a lot of residencies and awards, and now the Rakow Commission. How do you feel about that? What's the impact of receiving these kinds of awards on your work, or on your career, or on yourself?*

RS: Receiving the Rakow Commission is the most honorable award in my life so far. Installation work is very hard to make because I need space, you need to talk with the space, and you need to concentrate and change how you design your work into that space. It's a lot of work, but I want to try what I usually cannot do here. The Rakow Commission gives me the opportunity to do what I wanted to do for a long time, but I couldn't do it so far. It's really a great alternative to me to break in my limitation, what I can do myself.

An hour-long lecture by Rui Sasaki, "Meet the 2018 Rakow Commission Artist," is also available on the Museum's Web site and YouTube channel.

ABOUT THE RAKOW COMMISSION

Inaugurated in 1986 by The Corning Museum of Glass, the Rakow Commission supports the development of new works of art in glass, engaging artists whose works are of superior intellectual and/or technical quality that transcends the traditional boundaries of glassworking. Each commissioned work is added to the Museum's collection.

Since its inception, this program has provided an annual award to an artist, which is made possible through the generosity of the late Dr. and Mrs. Leonard S. Rakow, who were Fellows, friends, and benefactors of the Museum. Over the years, recipients of the Rakow Commission have ranged from emerging to established artists. Currently, the commission is awarded to artists whose work is not yet represented in the Museum's collection. Commissions are nominated by the curator of modern and contemporary glass, and selected by the Museum's acquisitions committee. Additional information on the commission is available on the Museum's Web site.

Artists who have received the Rakow Commission:

RUI SASAKI 2018

KARLYN SUTHERLAND 2017

THADDEUS WOLFE 2016

BERNHARD SCHOBINGER 2015

AMBER COWAN 2014

ANDREW ERDOS 2013

STEFFEN DAM 2012

ANN GARDNER 2011

LUKE JERRAM 2010

ISABEL DE OBALDÍA 2009

ZORA PALOVÁ 2008

DEBORA MOORE 2007

TIM EDWARDS 2006

NICOLE CHESNEY 2005

SILVIA LEVENSON 2004

PRESTON SINGLETARY 2003

JILL REYNOLDS 2002

YOICHI OHIRA 2001

JOSIAH McELHENY 2000

KLAUS MOJE 1999

MICHAEL SCHEINER 1998

ANN WOLFF 1997

LINO TAGLIAPIETRA 1996

JIŘÍ HARCUBA 1995

URSULA HUTH 1994

FRITZ DREISBACH 1993

JACQUELINE LILLIE 1992

HIROSHI YAMANO 1991

LYUBOV IVANOVNA SAVELYEVA 1990

DIANA HOBSON 1989

TOOTS ZYNSKY 1988

HOWARD BEN TRÉ 1987

DOUG ANDERSON 1986

FULGURITE

by Harbeer Sandhu

A play after PLATO, THORNTON WILDER, ANTONIN ARTAUD,
THE GODS MUST BE CRAZY, and too many issues
of NEW GLASS REVIEW

CHARACTERS: ARTIST
                CRITIC
                CURATOR
                HOUSEWARES BLOGGER
                      [Collectively, the PANEL]
                ROSE, the OFFICE MANAGER
                WORKERS [Four total]
                ANNOUNCER [Offstage, heard through the house PA]

ACT I

[A slideshow is PROJECTED on the house CURTAIN]

ANNOUNCER: And now, the management of the theater takes
pleasure in bringing you . . . The NEWS OF THE WORLD!

WASHINGTON, D.C.: GOVERNMENT is still at a STANDSTILL, with
partisans on both sides locked in a dualistic failure of
imagination, unable to conceive of any possibilities beyond
the most simplistic, with an ossified status quo limiting the
terms of any debate.

TIPPEHATCHEE, PENNSYLVANIA: The unprecedented hot weather of
this summer has produced a condition that has not yet been
explained. A great, churning, inland, hurricane-type cell of
THUNDERSTORMS formed over the Great Lakes and is moving east,
toward the Finger Lakes region of New York. Check your
cellphones for the latest alerts.

CORNING, NEW YORK: THE CORNING MUSEUM OF GLASS. An upcoming
INTERNATIONAL SURVEY of contemporary art and design IN GLASS
has centered the world's attention on this fine institution.
This unfortunately waterlogged week, its new[ish] CURATOR has
invited several authorities on glass to select just 100 pieces
from an open call that reportedly yielded no less than ONE
MILLION SLIDES representing work ranging from students to
hobbyists to established professionals and even commercial
manufacturers! Talk about a difficult job!

Now, let's meet the PANEL!

First off, the aforementioned CURATOR comes from good stock
and has made her way up from next to nothing. A good,

no-nonsense, All-American force of nature, she! [If not a tad overambitious, but like I said--All-American!]

This is the ARTIST, currently Chair of the Glass Studies Department at Antwerp Polytechnic. She is a trailblazing glass sculptor in her own right [and formerly an Artist in Residence right here at the Corning Institute]! It is she who invented the paperweight, on which so many interesting changes have been wrought since then.

Here we see MR. CRITIC, a man of many opinions. A passionate defender of abstraction in its many manifestations, MR. CRITIC is best known for his weekly column, "No, Your Kid Could Not Have Done That," which is syndicated in 144 local newspapers across our great country--that's a gross! MR. CRITIC is also the only juror to have sat on the panel for all three iterations of the Corning international survey exhibitions-- in 1959, 1979, and now again in 2019!

And finally, from Las Vegas, Nevada, meet the final member of this year's esteemed PANEL, the HOUSEWARES BLOGGER. If anybody understands the potential harmony from a perfect marriage of form and function, it's our HOUSEWARES BLOGGER--just ask her 45 million followers on SnapGram!

Here is a group shot of the full PANEL, taken in the new Contemporary Art + Design Wing of the Museum on the evening before they begin their deliberations. Don't they look so happy and . . . innocent? Note the BRIGHT RED LINE on the wall, labeled "1972 High Water Line," in memory of the infamous, catastrophic FLASH FLOOD of the Chemung River, which claimed 18 lives in Corning.

The FINGER in that final frame belongs to ROSE, OFFICE MANAGER of the Curatorial Department and the longest-running employee of The Corning Museum of Glass. It is ROSE who took these wonderful photos. And now, we bring you into the INTERIOR of the SEMINAR ROOM of the RAKOW RESEARCH LIBRARY, where deliberations will begin soon.

[SCREEN RISES to reveal the interior of the SEMINAR ROOM--an obsidian cave with obsidian stalactites and stalagmites. THREE WORKERS, DRESSED ALL IN BLACK--with BLACK TURTLENECKS, DARK GLASSES, and PLATINUM BLOND WIGS--tend a BONFIRE that stands before a 200-INCH, HONEYCOMB-BACKED MIRROR. The mirror focuses the firelight into a narrow beam that passes through a metal,

Day 1: The Beginning

View-Master-type SLIDE REEL before casting a BRIGHT SQUARE ON THE
OPPOSING WALL of the cave. A FOURTH WORKER SITS on a STATIONARY
BICYCLE, which powers a BELLOWS that feeds air to the fire and
TURNS THE SLIDE REEL. ROSE PACES ANXIOUSLY and FUSSES with files
and pastries on a table while directing her WORKERS.]

ROSE: Oh, oh, oh! Ten minutes 'til nine o'clock, and the
Curator's still not here yet. I sure hope nothing serious
happened to her crossing the Chemung--there's all that new
construction, and what with all this rain. . . . Her hybrid
doesn't exactly have the highest clearance. If anything
happened to her, why, we'd never get this show done in
time . . . and today she's got the Panel with her to boot,
all in that tiny hybrid. . . .

CURTAIN

ACT II

DAY ONE, MORNING

[CURTAIN RISES to reveal THREE MEMBERS of the PANEL SHACKLED TO
CHAIRS, shackled by their legs and necks, shackled so they cannot
turn their heads. With their EYELIDS CLAMPED OPEN, they have no
choice but to look straight ahead at the only thing they can see:
a BLANK SCREEN upon which a team of WORKERS PROJECT IMAGES from
behind the chairs where the PANEL are seated, such that those in
shackles are unable to see the source of the projections. The
CURATOR WALKS ABOUT freely and HOLDS in her hand a DEVICE THAT
JOLTS the WORKERS with a shock that STARTLES them, ADVANCING the
projection to the NEXT IMAGE.

We open with the CURATOR quickly advancing through the images
before the rest of the PANEL can even take them in.]

CURATOR: Next! Cut. Next! Cut. Next! Cut. . . . .

ARTIST: Wait, wait, wait, wait! Back up a second!

CURATOR [to WORKERS]: Wait, wait, wait, wait! Back up a
second!

254

[WORKERS SCURRY and FUMBLE with projector. Sound of a HEAVY WHEEL slowing down, CREAKING to a halt, then slowly regaining momentum.]

ARTIST [to CURATOR]: Would you be upset if. . . .

CURATOR [to ARTIST]: Yes?

ARTIST: You would? Be upset?

CURATOR: I don't know, you haven't asked me a complete question yet.

ARTIST: Never mind. I can see that you're upset.

CURATOR: I'm not. Trust me. It's fine. What is it?

CRITIC: Come along now, friend, don't be shy. This is why we came here, after all!

ARTIST [haltingly]: OK, if you say so. What I was going to ask is . . . would you mind if I brought the snow globe back?

BLOGGER: The snow globe?

CURATOR: The snow globe?

CRITIC: Do you mean the paperweight? With the barn?

CURATOR: You must mean the paperweight! With the barn!

ARTIST: Yes! The paperweight! With the barn!

CURATOR: Of course not! WORKERS! BRING BACK THE PAPERWEIGHT WITH THE BARN!

BLOGGER: Twenty-four centimeters. How many inches is that?

CRITIC: In that case, can I bring back the purple neon piece?

ARTIST: Twenty-four centimeters is about ten inches. *Day 1: Morning*

CURATOR: Do what you want, but note that we are just at the beginning of the process. On the first pass, let's let doubt weigh on the side of keeping it; on the second viewing, our doubts should work against it.

BLOGGER: Ten inches?! How big is your paper if you need
a ten-inch paperweight? Can anybody even lift such a
paperweight?

CRITIC: Perhaps it's a conceptual paperweight.

BLOGGER: You mean a mock functional object? Like a glass tire?

CRITIC: Not quite. I mean, in a sense, but so much more
than that. It contains a barn, a barn inside a substantial
amount of glass, which must magnify whatever is on the
paper beneath.

ARTIST: It's like the barn in THE WIZARD OF OZ! Crushing the
Wicked Witch--which would be whatever oppressive papers lie
beneath. . . .

BLOGGER: I don't know. I feel pretty strongly that even
though function need have no relation to appearance, the
visual aspect should nonetheless be subordinate to function.
A goblet must "feel" right in the hand; a group of cooking
utensils must be easy to clean and to store in the cupboard;
a teapot must have the handle placed so that the pot will be
balanced when it pours.

CRITIC: If only the photographer had included another object
in the frame to provide a sense of scale.

ARTIST: Look, if anybody knows paperweights, it's me.
I invented. . . .

CRITIC: And does it need to be in glass? Does being in glass
add anything to the object, mock functional or sincerely
functional? It's always a fair question to ask what difference
its being in glass makes to a work. What meaning is contributed
by the fact that glass is used? The quality of material may
be breathtaking, the technique pure wizardry, and the result
a bore.

CURATOR: Technique is cheap. As much has been done in butter
and ice without reflecting glory on the materials.

ARTIST: Technique is cheap, cheap, cheap. Technique is cheap,
cheap, cheap! What kind of bird am I?

CRITIC: But think of Cinderella's glass slipper--something as
fragile and iridescent as the ornaments on the Christmas tree,

pressed into romantic but stressful service as celebratory
footwear, where by all rights it should shatter into dangerous
shards the moment the young lady takes her first step.

[THUNDER CRACKS. The stage LIGHTS FLICKER. Off in the distance,
a WEATHER SIREN BLARES, as ALARMS GO OFF on each member of the
PANEL's PHONE. Another FLASH and a simultaneous THUNDER CRACK
indicate the storm's close proximity. WIND HOWLS from what sounds
like the outside of the theater and makes the long passageway down
to the cave resonate like someone blowing over the mouth of a glass
bottle. ROSE approaches the CURATOR and WHISPERS IN HER EAR.]

    CURATOR: Lunch!

[TAKEOUT MENUS RAIN DOWN like CONFETTI as the CURTAIN FALLS.]

                        ACT III

                   DAY ONE, AFTERNOON

[The CURTAIN RISES to show THREE WORKERS FEEDING the shackled and
bound MEMBERS of the PANEL. WATER begins to DRIP from the ceiling.
The WORKERS finish feeding the PANEL and PLACE PAILS beneath the
leaks. METALLIC PINGS randomly punctuate the following scene.]

    CURATOR: Next! Cut. Next! Cut. . . .   *Day 1: Afternoon*
_____

    BLOGGER: Do we have any submissions from the Hotshot with
    the Ascot?

    CURATOR: Nope. He either thinks he's too big for a group show
    or he's afraid that we'd reject him. Next! Cut.

    BLOGGER: How about Brittany Studios? Their lampshades are
    making a comeback. Also, my eyes are terribly dry. Is anybody
    else having trouble with their eyes?

    CURATOR: Non. Cut. Only one factory submitted a single thing,
    and even that under the designer's name, not the factory's.
    Next!

    ARTIST: How about Hippy Longstalkings? And yes, I've been
    crying about my eyes since the morning.

CURATOR: Yes, but not the piece I asked for. She's way into her new stuff, but it's not quite there yet. I still like her older stuff. Next!

[THUNDER and LIGHTNING. MORE LEAKS APPEAR, and the leaks get faster. WORKERS SLIP and SCURRY, adding more PAILS, which get LOUDER. The PANEL members RAISE THEIR VOICES to compete with the din as the scene progresses.]

BLOGGER: Bup, bup, wait, hold on, pause. Are those pipes? I've heard a lot about these glass pipes, ever since WEEDS, all these housewives, with their dabs and torches and glass bongs.

[A SLIDE shows three plain cylindrical pitchers made of thick, transparent, lightly tinted glass. Each bears a cylindrical spout of a different color protruding from its body, near the top.]

CURATOR: Do you mean these pitchers?

CRITIC: Well, actually, this is clearly not a pipe. One can easily imagine the pleasure of pouring amber-colored brandy from this gay and companionable bottle, which, because of its appropriate and sensitive design, makes an addition to the party in its own right.

ARTIST: I could go for a brandy; it's freezing in here! But why do you talk like some staid, 1950s academic? And can we do something about our eyes, please?! Mine are blurring over. I think I'm developing cataracts.

ROSE [WHISPERING LOUDLY to ARTIST]: Don't you know this whole text is plagiarized from past issues of NEW GLASS REVIEW?! He's a pastiche of all the stuffy male panelists over the years.

CURATOR [SPEAKING OVER ROSE]: Workers! Please scooch each member of the panel to beneath a leak, lest their eyes dry out.

ARTIST: Ooh, I've never been Chinese water-tortured before!

[MORE THUNDER and LIGHTNING as the LEAKS GROW FASTER and the PAILS GET LOUDER.]

BLOGGER: I don't know. . . . Don't you find them a little . . . obscene? Those protuberances? I mean, you know, in light of

current circumstances. . . . "Just grab 'em by the spout"
like?

CRITIC: Vessels of the Han would not show more balanced or
satisfying form.

BLOGGER: Where would you put your mouth, anyway? On the
spout? Obscene, I tell you.

ARTIST: Thirty centimeters. How many inches is that, again?

BLOGGER: And the . . . "tobacco." Where would the "tobacco" go?

CRITIC [to BLOGGER]: Again, I assure you, it is not a
pipe! [To ARTIST] You're the one who lives in Belgium!
Why are you asking for the metric conversion?

Day 2: Morning

ARTIST: Wacky tobacky, ha!

CURATOR [GROANS]: Everybody take five. Smoke break!

CURTAIN

ACT IV

DAY TWO, MORNING

[Image of RAIN and the WORKERS and PANEL arriving at the Rakow
Research Library by BOAT on a swollen Chemung River, after
Leutze's WASHINGTON CROSSING THE DELAWARE.]

ANNOUNCER: The following day. As the rainstorm continues
unabated and floodwaters rise, members of the PANEL, freed
from their shackles, begin the final round of deliberations.

CURTAIN RISES

CURATOR: ROSE has taped printouts of the remaining slides
on the walls of this obsidian cave--I mean, the Seminar Room
of the Rakow Research Library. You should each have some

25 color-coded stickers. Please just place your stickers on
the pieces you support.

[Members of the PANEL begin a kind of silent MODERN DANCE
performance, MOVING ABOUT the space and PLACING STICKERS on their
choices. Throughout this movement, RAINWATER LOUDLY continues
DRIPPING from the stalactites into metal pails as more WATER RISES
UP from the depths. From this rising water bubbles up a curious
OBJECT that HITS one of the pails with a CLANG that CATCHES
EVERYBODY'S ATTENTION.]

> ARTIST: What the . . . ? [TAPS it with a FINGERNAIL.]

> CRITIC: It's a. . . . [TAPS it with a PENCIL.]

> CURATOR: Let me see! [TURNS IT in the light, NEAR HER FACE,
> then at ARM'S LENGTH.]

> BLOGGER [GRABS IT and BLOWS over a narrow opening near its top]:
> It's an instrument, a musical instrument.

> CRITIC [SNATCHES IT and STICKS HIS FINGER IN IT, which GETS
> STUCK]: Pull my finger?

> CURATOR [GRABS hold of it and PULLS. It goes FLYING and lands
> in the rising waters with a SPLASH]: Now look what you've
> done!

> CRITIC: This thing, this object, it is so much *realer* than
> any slide. It shows such pleasure in the material itself.
> I want to touch it, to turn it around, to explore its shapes
> and shadows.

> ARTIST: It's so obviously simple, without ornament . . . or
> fuss.

> BLOGGER: Ha! I thought you were describing yourself, until
> the end there.

[WATER has risen to CHEST LEVEL by this point.]

> CURATOR: We are almost done, folks. Could we just stay on
> task, please?

> CRITIC: Delicate in its material, graceful in its shape, and
> dignified and aristocratic in its posture--the kind of object
> that lends dignity to the objects around it.

ARTIST: I'm pretty sure it's just a Coke bottle, chief.
It's not like it's a paperweight. Gosh, you take yourself
seriously!

CRITIC: Whatever it is, I find its delight and flavor in its
glassiness. It is heavy in the hand, a lot of glass. The light
plays in and through it and around its irregular smooth
surfaces, acting exactly as light should in glass. It refines
the light that it absorbs and sends it back magnified,
controlled, and converted into a new, confined but fluid sort
of microcosm.

[WATER is at NECK LEVEL.]

CURATOR: ROSE! Quick! I don't know if we will make it, but the
show must go on! Take down all the remaining pages and seal
them in this bottle.

ROSE: Whatever you say, boss! [She GATHERS SHEETS and SEALS
THEM IN THE BOTTLE, just as FLOODWATERS RUSH IN and DROWN the
PANEL while CARRYING THE BOTTLE OFF IN THE CURRENT.]

CURTAIN

THE END

HARBEER SANDHU writes fiction, lyrical essays, and art criticism,
and is a 2013 recipient of an ARTS WRITERS GRANT from THE ANDY
WARHOL FOUNDATION and CREATIVE CAPITAL.

Recent Important Acquisitions

from Collections Worldwide

This section consists of photographs and descriptions of objects recently added to public and private collections in the United States and abroad. All of these objects, which are arranged alphabetically by institution and then by artist, were made between 1946 and the present. They include glass design, craft, sculpture, installations, and architectural projects. Mixed-media art works are included only if a significant part of the work is made of glass. Caption information has been provided by the owners.

Village of Fallen Flowers
1988
KYOHEI FUJITA (Japanese,
1921–2004)

Mold-blown glass, applied gold and
platinum leaf; silver lip wraps

12.7 x 17.8 x 17.8 cm

The Baltimore Museum of Art,
Baltimore, Maryland (2017.163, gift of
Linda and G. Arnold Kaufman)

Photo: Courtesy of The Baltimore
Museum of Art

Untitled (Hexagon Sculpture)
Iran, 2013
MONIR FARMANFARMAIAN
(Iranian, b. 1924)

Cut mirror mosaic and plaster
on wood

60.9 x 71.1 x 71.1 cm

Barry Art Museum, Old Dominion
University, Norfolk, Virginia (2018.9,
Carolyn K. Barry and Richard F.
Barry III Art Purchase Fund)

Photo: Courtesy of Haines Gallery

Dove
Czechoslovakia, Karlovy Vary, 1980
STANISLAV LIBENSKÝ (Czech, 1921–2001)

Made by Moser Glass

Cast colorless glass, cut, polished, assembled

297.2 x 114.3 x 78.7 cm

Barry Art Museum, Old Dominion University, Norfolk, Virginia (2018.11, Carolyn K. Barry and Richard F. Barry III Art Purchase Fund)

Photo: Courtesy of Charles Thomas, senior photographer, Old Dominion University

Passage #5
2014
MARK PEISER (American, b. 1938)

Hot-cast phase-separated glass; cast glass base

86.4 x 31.8 x 19.1 cm

Barry Art Museum, Old Dominion University, Norfolk, Virginia (2017.105, gift of Carolyn K. Barry and Richard F. Barry III)

Photo: Courtesy of Dave Chance Photography

Great Dismal Swamp
2018
SIBYLLE PERETTI
(German, b. 1964)

Kiln-formed opaline glass, engraved, painted, silvered; paper appliqué

152.4 x 203.2 x 1.3 cm

Barry Art Museum, Old Dominion University, Norfolk, Virginia (2018.10, Carolyn K. Barry and Richard F. Barry III Art Purchase Fund)

Photo: Courtesy of Heller Gallery, NY

Untitled Vessel
United States, 1963
HARVEY K. LITTLETON
(American, 1922–2013)

Blown glass

21 x 13.3 x 13.3 cm

Chrysler Museum of Art, Norfolk, Virginia (2018.18, gift of Corey and Regina Hampson)

Photo: Ed Pollard, Chrysler Museum of Art

Turmoil
Republic of South Africa,
KwaZulu-Natal, Ubuhle
Women collective, 2018

ZANDILE NTOBELA
(Xhosa [South African], b. 1986)

Czech glass beads on fabric

141.2 x 67.3 cm

Chrysler Museum of Art, Norfolk,
Virginia (2018.37.1, museum
purchase)

Photo: Ed Pollard, Chrysler Museum
of Art

Kachina 2
Italy, 2006

ETTORE SOTTSASS
(Italian, 1917–2007)

Blown glass

41.9 x 43.8 cm

Chrysler Museum of Art, Norfolk,
Virginia (2017.40.1, museum purchase
with funds provided by Pat and Doug
Perry, Michael Bakwin, Lisa S.
and Dudley B. Anderson, Jim Hixon,
Suzanne and Vince Mastracco, Joe
Waldo and Ashby Vail, Pat and Colin
McKinnon, Carolyn and Dick Barry,
Charlotte and Gil Minor, and Selina
and Tom Stokes)

Photo: Ed Pollard, Chrysler Museum
of Art

VFZ 1
United States, Venice and Van Nuys, California, 2017

LARRY BELL (American, b. 1939)

Laminated UV glass, colored PET film, silicon epoxy

182.9 x 243.8 x 243.8 cm

The Corning Museum of Glass, Corning, New York (2018.4.13, purchased in part with special funds provided by Corning Incorporated in honor of the opening of the Contemporary Art + Design Wing, March 2015)

Speckled Suction Cups
United States, Wheaton, New Jersey, and Brooklyn, New York, 2017

ALISON SIEGEL
(American, b. 1987)
and PAMELA SABROSO
(American, b. Venezuela, 1982)

Mold-blown and lampworked glass, hot-worked, cold-worked, assembled; mussel shell

21.4 x 13.2 x 11.6 cm

The Corning Museum of Glass, Corning, New York (2018.4.12)

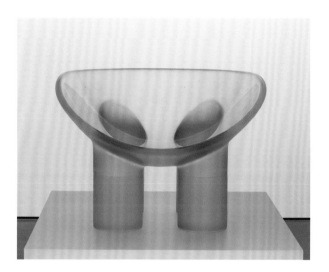

Roly-Poly Chair/Water
Designed in the United Kingdom,
London, England, 2015, and made
in the Czech Republic, 2018
FAYE TOOGOOD (British, b. 1977)

Kiln-cast lithium-barium glass

58.5 x 85 x 63 cm

The Corning Museum of Glass,
Corning, New York (2018.3.9)

Mining Industries: Corning
United States, Plainwell, Michigan,
2018
NORWOOD VIVIANO
(American, b. 1972)

Kiln-cast glass from 3-D-printed
model; steel, mirrored glass,
transparencies

48 x 85 x 58 cm

The Corning Museum of Glass,
Corning, New York (2018.4.10, gift
of James B. Flaws and Marcia D.
Weber)

Virgin and Child Glass Panel
United Kingdom, England, about 1958

JOHN HUTTON
(British, b. New Zealand, 1906–1978)

Wheel-engraved glass

71.3 x 41.5 cm

The Fitzwilliam Museum, University of Cambridge, Cambridge, England, United Kingdom (C.2-2018, gift of Jacob Simon)

Photo: Courtesy of The Fitzwilliam Museum, © Estate of John Hutton

Window_3
Great Britain, 2014

ERIN DICKSON (British, b. 1987)

Waterjet-cut glass, fused

71 x 60 x 2 cm

Glasmuseet Ebeltoft, Ebeltoft, Denmark (774-1, prize winner, Young Glass 2017 competition)

Photo: David Williams

Weather Chandelier
2015
RUI SASAKI (Japanese, b. 1984)
Blown glass, cold-worked
55 x 70 cm
Glasmuseet Ebeltoft, Ebeltoft,
Denmark (741-2, prize winner,
Young Glass 2017 competition)
Photo: Kiichiro Okamura

Loss
2015
KATHRYN WIGHTMAN
(British, b. 1983)
Screen-printed glass powders on
sheet glass, kiln-formed
38 x 83 x 0.6 cm
Glasmuseet Ebeltoft, Ebeltoft,
Denmark (773-1, prize winner,
Young Glass 2017 competition)
Photo: Courtesy of the artist

Herz aus Glas
Germany, 1969
ERWIN EISCH (German, b. 1927)
Blown glass, covered with platinum
17 x 15.5 cm
Kunstsammlungen der Veste Coburg–European Museum of Modern Glass, Coburg, Germany (a.S.6174, acquired with a gift of Rolf Schmidt, Coburg)
Photo: Courtesy of Kunstsammlungen der Veste Coburg

Vase
Czechoslovakia, 1964
RENÉ ROUBÍČEK (Czech, 1922–2018)
Blown glass
20 x 28 cm
Kunstsammlungen der Veste Coburg–European Museum of Modern Glass, Coburg, Germany (a.S.6094)
Photo: Courtesy of Kunstsammlungen der Veste Coburg

Freezer
Germany, 2017
JULIUS WEILAND
(German, b. 1971)

Blown and fused glass

33 x 28 cm

Kunstsammlungen der Veste Coburg–European Museum of Modern Glass, Coburg, Germany (a.S.6090)

Photo: Courtesy of Kunstsammlungen der Veste Coburg, © Julius Weiland, VG BILD-KUNST, Bonn

Measuring Cups
2014
MARIE-HÉLÈNE BEAULIEU
(Canadian, b. 1979)
and SÉBASTIEN DUCHANGE
(French, b. 1977)

Blown borosilicate glass, cut, polished; gold

Dimensions vary

The Montreal Museum of Fine Arts, Montreal, Quebec, Canada (2018.192, MMFA purchase, Ruth Jackson Bequest)

Photo: Courtesy of The Montreal Museum of Fine Arts

Assemblage
2016
THADDEUS WOLFE
(American, b. 1979)

Mold-blown glass, cold-worked

25.4 x 10.8 x 10 cm

The Montreal Museum of Fine Arts, Montreal, Quebec, Canada (2018.76, MMFA purchase, Suzanne Caouette Bequest)

Photo: Courtesy of The Montreal Museum of Fine Arts

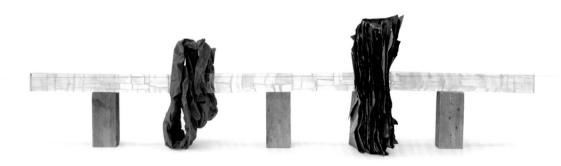

X-Press
France, 2015

MARTINE PERRIN (French, b. 1949)
and JACKI PERRIN (French, b. 1943)

"Build-in" glass, Cristal of Saint-Louis;
wood, paper

55 x 360 x 35 cm

Musée du Verre de Charleroi,
Marcinelle, Belgium (MDV inv. 4582)

Photo: S. Briolant

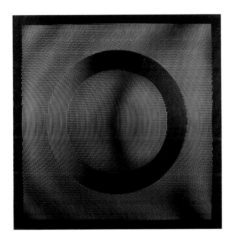

Harey II.
Hungary, Budapest, 2014
ZSUZSANNA KÓRÓDI
(Hungarian, b. 1984)

Laminated, ground, and silk-printed sheet glass

50 x 50 x 1 cm

Museum of Applied Arts, Budapest, Hungary (2018.15.1.)

Photo: Krisztina Friedrich

Quiet Shifting, Blue and Green
Quiet Shifting, Pink and Green
Australia, Adelaide, South Australia, 2018

CLARE BELFRAGE
(Australian, b. 1966)

Blown glass with cane drawing, sandblasted, pumice-polished

Larger: 56 x 39 x 26 cm

Museum of Applied Arts and Sciences, Sydney, New South Wales, Australia (2018/108/1-2, purchased with funds from the Barry Willoughby Bequest, 2018)

Photo: Marinco Kojdanovski, MAAS

Gorgonia 15
("Coral Works" Series)
United States, Provincetown,
Massachusetts, 2018
TIMOTHY HORN
(Australian, b. 1964)

Mirrored blown glass; nickel-plated
cast bronze

214 x 228 x 24 cm

*Museum of Applied Arts and
Sciences*, Sydney, New South Wales,
Australia (2018/40/1, purchased with
funds from the Barry Willoughby
Bequest, 2018)

Photo: Marinco Kojdanovski, MAAS

Laid (Time-) Table with Cycads
United States, Sheboygan Falls,
Wisconsin, 2015

BETH LIPMAN (American, b. 1971)

Glass, adhesive, wood, paint

233.7 x 487.7 x 144.8 cm

Museum of Arts and Design, New
York, New York (gift of the Kohler
Foundation Inc., 2018)

Photo: Courtesy of the artist

Cosmic Elixir: Sun Ra's "Love in Outer Space," Distilled May 27, 2018, Bottle 14*

United States, Brooklyn, New York, 2018

JOSIAH McELHENY

(American, b. 1966)

Blown glass

35.5 x 10 cm

Museum of Arts and Design, New York, New York (purchased with funds provided by the Collections Committee, 2018)

Photo: Courtesy of Corbett vs. Dempsey

*Bottle 70 is illustrated here.

Fancy Footed Osage

United States, Brooklyn, New York, 2017

ALISON SIEGEL

(American, b. 1987)

and PAMELA SABROSO

(American, b. Venezuela, 1982)

Blown, cast, and flameworked glass, assembled

29.2 x 17.8 x 19.1 cm

Museum of Arts and Design, New York, New York (purchased with funds provided by the Collections Committee, 2018)

Photo: Courtesy of Heller Gallery

Unique Assemblage Vessel
United States, 2015

THADDEUS WOLFE
(American, b. 1979)

Mold-blown glass, cold-worked

24.8 x 14 x 11.4 cm

The Museum of Fine Arts, Houston,
Houston, Texas (2018.67, museum
purchase funded by the bequest of
Arthur Robson Jr. in honor of Claire
and Robert T. Lober)

Photo: Thomas R. DuBrock,
© The Museum of Fine Arts, Houston

RedPrint #0476
2008

MATTHEW CURTIS
(British/Australian, b. 1964)

Blown glass, etched

35.6 x 25.4 x 17.8 cm

Museum of Glass, Tacoma,
Washington (2017.13, gift
of Dr. Dennis Chugh)

Photo: Duncan Price

Shelter Series
1988
RICHARD ROYAL
(American, b. 1952)
Blown and sculpted glass
22.9 x 69.9 x 22.9 cm
Museum of Glass, Tacoma,
Washington (TR.2018.4, gift
of Tim and Craig Kelly)
Photo: Duncan Price

Architectures / Solitudes
Slovakia, 2015
PALO MACHO (Slovakian, b. 1965)
Painted and fused glass
54 x 42 x 12 cm
MusVerre, Sars-Poteries, France
(2018.1.1)
Photo: Paul Louis

Ingewikkeld
Belgium, 2017
CHRISTINE VANOPPEN
(Belgian, b. 1962)
Flameworked glass
25 x 70 cm
MusVerre, Sars-Poteries,
France (2017.15.1)
Photo: Paul Louis

Fusion
France and Germany, 2018
UDO ZEMBOK (French, b. 1951)
Fused glass
320 x 140 x 20 cm
MusVerre, Sars-Poteries,
France (2018.3.1)
Photo: Courtesy of MusVerre

Pink Tercet
United States, New York, New York,
about 1985

SYDNEY CASH (American, b. 1941)

Slumped glass

17.8 x 19.1 x 19.1 cm

Philadelphia Museum of Art,
Philadelphia, Pennsylvania
(2017-18-1, gift of Mrs. Robert L.
McNeil Jr., 2017)

Photo: Juan Arce, PMA Digital
Photography, 2018

Sheep Bowl ("Cylinder" Series)
United States, Stanwood,
Washington, 1982

FLORA MACE (American, b. 1949)
and JOEY KIRKPATRICK
(American, b. 1952)

Blown glass, etched

18.4 x 22.9 cm

Philadelphia Museum of Art,
Philadelphia, Pennsylvania
(2017-102-5, gift of Adam Kamens
in memory of Sy Kamens, 2017)

Photo: Juan Arce, PMA Digital
Photography, 2018

Resplendent
Japan, 2017
MIDORI TSUKADA
(Japanese, b. 1972)

Fused and molded glass

19.7 x 11.4 x cm

Philadelphia Museum of Art,
Philadelphia, Pennsylvania
(2018-111-1, purchased with funds
contributed by Barbara L. Phillips,
2018)

Photo: Courtesy Philadelphia
Museum of Art, Joseph Hu.

Venetian Vessel
1993
DALE CHIHULY
(American, b. 1941)

Blown glass

47.6 x 43.2 cm

Racine Art Museum, Racine,
Wisconsin (IR2018.136, gift
of Dale and Doug Anderson)

Photo: Jon Bolton

Art vs. Craft: Reversible Goblet (AKA A Tribute to Will Rogers, A Ropin' Fool)
1982
FRITZ DREISBACH
(American, b. 1941)

Blown glass

25.4 x 23.5 x 12.1 cm

Racine Art Museum, Racine, Wisconsin (IR2017.252, gift of Alan and Barbara Boroff and the Kohler Foundation Inc.)

Photo: Jon Bolton

Current
United States, Seattle, Washington, 1994
MARTIN BLANK
(American, b. 1962)

Slumped glass; reclaimed wood, metal

Dimensions vary

Tacoma Art Museum, Tacoma, Washington (2018.2, gift of Rosalind B. Poll)

Photo: Terry Rishel

Object No. 23
2018
STINE BIDSTRUP (Danish, b. 1982)

Mold-blown glass with digitally enhanced Graal technique

24.8 x 36.8 x 30.8 cm

Toledo Museum of Art, Toledo, Ohio (PC2018.30.01)

Photo: Courtesy of the Heller Gallery

Aram ("Convertible" Series)
2015
MONIR FARMANFARMAIAN
(Iranian, b. 1924)

Mirror, reverse painting on glass, plaster on wood

195.6 x 195.6 x 2.5 cm

Toledo Museum of Art, Toledo, Ohio (2018.15A–F, purchased with funds from the Florence Scott Libbey Bequest in memory of her father, Maurice A. Scott)

Photo: Richard Goodbody

Companion Species (Repose)
United States, Corning, New York,
The Corning Museum of Glass, 2017
MARIE WATT (American, b. 1967)
Solid crystal on Western walnut
22.9 x 58.4 x 26.7 cm
Toledo Museum of Art, Toledo, Ohio
(2018.41, purchased with funds given
by Dr. Loren Lipson)
Photo: Richard Goodbody

Korb V
Germany, 2014
MONA HATOUM
(Palestinian, b. Lebanon, 1952)
Blown glass; steel
33 x 49.5 x 45 cm
Alexander Tutsek-Stiftung,
Munich, Germany
Photo: Joerg Lohse, © Mona
Hatoum, courtesy of Alexander
and Bonin, New York

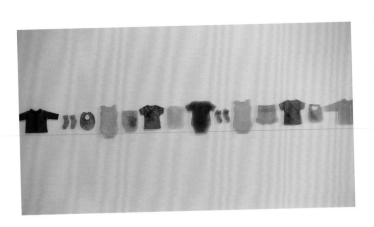

Identidad Recuperada/
Recovered Identity (detail)
Italy, 2014–2018
SILVIA LEVENSON
(Argentinian, b. 1957)
Kiln-cast glass (128 pieces)
Dimensions vary
Alexander Tutsek-Stiftung,
Munich, Germany
Photo: Marco del Comune,
© Silvia Levenson

Marseille Template/16
France, 2004–2006
TERRY WINTERS
(American, b. 1949)
Blown glass; wood
75 x 34 x 34 cm
Alexander Tutsek-Stiftung,
Munich, Germany
Photo: © Terry Winters, courtesy
of Matthew Marks Gallery

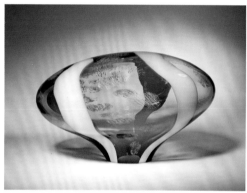

Dichotomy
United Kingdom, 2018
HARRY MORGAN (British, b. 1990)
Concrete, pulled glass threads
92 x 31 x 31 cm
Victoria and Albert Museum,
Ceramics & Glass Section, London,
England, United Kingdom (Prov.474-
2018, museum purchase)
Photo: Courtesy of the Victoria and
Albert Museum, London

Stone V
United States, 2017
ANN WÅHLSTRÖM (Swedish, b.
1957)
Blown colorless-grayish glass with
opaque white "filigree" inclusions
25 x 41 x 33 cm
Victoria and Albert Museum,
Ceramics & Glass Section, London,
England, United Kingdom (C.6-2018,
museum purchase)
Photo: Courtesy of the Victoria and
Albert Museum, London

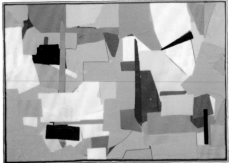

*View from Window
Western Ridge*
Australia, 2017
BRENDEN SCOTT FRENCH
(Australian, b. 1969)
Kiln-formed glass
109.5 x 78.5 x 0.4 cm
*Wagga Wagga Art Gallery–National
Art Glass Collection*, Wagga Wagga,
New South Wales, Australia
(2018.054a, b, purchase funded by
Wagga Wagga City Council)
Photo: Tayla Martin

Wax and Wane
Australia, 2018
THOMAS PEARSON
(Australian, b. 1993)
Blown glass; sand
Larger: 47 x 19 x 12 cm
*Wagga Wagga Art Gallery–National
Art Glass Collection*, Wagga Wagga,
New South Wales, Australia
(2018.015a, b, purchase funded by
Wagga Wagga City Council)
Photo: Pippi Mount